Safety
in
the Air

Safety in the Air

by
Maurice Allward

Abelard-Schuman · London · New York · Toronto

By the same author:

The Aircraft Industry
Air Travel
Do You Know About Aircraft?
Do You Know About Space Flight?
Inside a Jet Airliner
London's Airports
Milestones in Science
Objective Outer Space
Spitfire
Triumphs of the Air
Westland 50
Wings for Tomorrow
The World of Space

© Copyright 1967 by Maurice Allward
First published 1967
First published in the United States 1968
Library of Congress Catalog Card Number: 68–10339
Standard Book Number: 200. 71484. 8

LONDON: Abelard-Schuman Limited, 8 King Street WC2
NEW YORK: Abelard-Schuman Limited, 6 West 57 Street
TORONTO: Abelard-Schuman Canada Limited, 896 Queen Street
West

Contents

Contents

Illustrations

Illustrations

Acknowledgements

Safety in the air is essentially the interchange of knowledge between pilots, between airline operators, between aircraft manufacturers and between airworthiness authorities. This book on air safety would not have been possible without the generous help of many people and organizations, including:

George Hart, who gave valuable comments on and assistance with the manuscript at all stages of its preparation, and the

Air Registration Board
Air Safety Group
American Air Line Pilots Association
Board of Trade
Boeing Company
Braniff International Airways Inc.
British Aircraft Corporation
British Air Line Pilots Association
British European Airways
British Overseas Airways Corporation
Civil Aeronautics Board
Daniel and Florence Guggenheim Aviation Safety
   Center
Douglas Aircraft Co., Inc.
Federal Aviation Agency
Flight Safety Committee
Flight Safety Foundation
General Aviation Safety Committee
Guild of Air Pilots and Air Navigators
Hawker Siddeley Aviation

International Civil Aviation Organization
Kaman Aircraft Corporation
Monsanto Chemicals Ltd.
National Aeronautics and Space Administration
National Air Traffic Control Services
Royal Aircraft Establishment
Smiths Industries Ltd.
The Society of Licensed Aircraft Engineers and
Technologists,
    and finally,
my wife, Alice, who did all the typing.

There is one notable omission from those who contributed to this book – the authorities in the Soviet Union. There is no reason to suppose that the safety record of Aeroflot compares unfavourably with that of major Western airlines, and some information on the trend of those accidents which do occur, and the steps being taken to prevent their recurrence, would obviously be of interest generally. At the moment accidents involving Soviet aircraft are only reported if Western tourists are involved, or if the crash occurs outside the Soviet Union. Such reticence is not worthy of one of the younger Soviet enterprises and it is hoped that it will not be long before they "grow up" and freely interchange information on matters affecting safety.

Introduction

The object of this book is to explain the immense care and thought devoted to the matter of your safety in the air. This safety is ensured by thousands of governmental regulations, by the high standards in the design and manufacture of every component part of an aeroplane and by the rigid procedures of safety practices of airlines. However, because aircraft accidents are more spectacular than those of other forms of transport, air travel is often considered less safe than it really is. In fact, the risk taken by an ordinary airliner passenger is well within the risks of normal day-to-day living. Otherwise, airliner pilots would not be able to obtain life insurance cover for the same premiums as ordinary people.

Of all transport systems, the airline industry is the most safety-conscious. In no other form of transport are accidents investigated so thoroughly, the lessons learned more carefully or applied more widely. There has been a steady reduction in the accident rate, although the total number of casualties has risen as the number of people travelling by air has greatly increased.

For example, in Britain, over a five year period forty years ago, the death rate on scheduled services per 100 million passenger miles was 69, the total number of passengers killed during this period being 19. If this rate of 69 had continued until today, the total deaths over the last five years would have been over 17,000. Fortunately, the rate during this period was not 69, but 0.41 per 100 million passenger miles, and the passenger death roll was not 17,000, but just over 100.

The present risk is thus a hundred times better than it was forty years ago. However, there is no cause for complacency, particularly by British airlines, and the death rate must be reduced much further. If it is not, some air experts think that the anticipated growth of air travel will produce so many accidents that further expansion may be stopped or even reversed through the consequent bad publicity and public fear.

This matter of increasing air safety in the future forms the subject of the last chapter, titled "To safer flying". The thoughts of the major airworthiness authorities are analysed, and it is hoped that this portion of the book will be of interest not only to those whose safety is being ensured, but to those responsible for ensuring safety in the air.

Safety
in
the Air

1

How safe is air travel?

How safe is air travel? "Very safe," say the statisticians. "Very dangerous," thinks the public. Who is right? The answer is, both, depending on what you mean by "safe".

The "air travel is very safe" advocates point out, quite truthfully, that the number of passengers killed in aeroplanes is only a tiny fraction of those killed on the roads. But even if the numbers of travellers involved in each sphere were equal, and they are not, the comparison would not be a fair one, for most of the deaths on the roads involve amateur drivers and riders, some of whom are inexperienced or even downright irresponsible. Airline crews, on the other hand, are skilled professionals who have been subjected to a programme of selection, training and checking probably more intensive than that of any other body of men, while their aircraft are designed, built and maintained according to rules much stricter than those for motor-cars.

How is air safety measured? It can be assessed using a variety of yardsticks, each giving a part, but not all, of the picture. There is no universally satisfactory

yardstick. For example, an accepted supposition is
that the flying hazard is proportional to the number
of take-offs and landings: that is, the greater number
of take-offs and landings, the greater the likelihood of
an accident. However, contrary to this supposition, a
recent analysis of U.S. feeder airlines showed that on
this basis the feeders, with an average stage length of
only 90 miles, were about four times better than the
long-range operators with an average stage length of
1,100 miles.   Another common way of measuring
air safety is to determine the number of fatalities per
hours flown. On this basis the safety rate of the U.S.
feeder lines, previously indicated as being better than
that of long-haul operators, is only 0.7 as good. This
serves to emphasize how statistics can be used to prove
or disprove the safety of flying.

On the basis of millions of hours flown, the accident
record of jet airliners shows that in the first five million
hours there was a steady reduction, the number of
accidents in which the aircraft was a total loss being
9, 7, 6, 5 and 2 per million hours respectively. In the
sixth million hours the figure unfortunately rose to 5,
but dropped to 3 in the eighth million. These accidents
resulted in 190 passenger fatalities per million jet
hours, compared with an average of 73 passengers
killed per million hours on world-wide scheduled
services.

At the end of 1966 the total number of jet hours
flown was nearly seventeen million; at this time there
had been over 60 jet accidents involving the total
loss of the aircraft. On average then, there is one
accident in which the aircraft is lost every 260,000
flying hours. This can be compared with the figure

of one fatal accident every 300,000 hours for long-haul, piston-engined airliners, obtained over a ten-year period.

From the technical aspect experience has shown that there is not much to choose between the two yardsticks of flights and flying hours. Each has its own advantages depending upon what one wants to know. If one wants to measure the safety of landing gear, flights are more appropriate; but if one wants to measure the safety of engines, then hours are better.

The most widely used method of assessing the overall safety of a transport system is based on the number of fatalities experienced during so many passenger-miles. "Passenger-miles" is the number of passengers multiplied by the distance over which they are carried. Thus, a flight of 1,000 miles by an aeroplane carrying 100 passengers represents 100,000 passenger-miles. For convenience, air safety is usually considered on the basis of the number of fatalities per 100 million passenger-miles.

Table 1 shows the yearly safety statistics on this basis for the world's scheduled airlines (excluding the U.S.S.R. and China) from 1950 to 1966. The table lists the numbers of people killed each year, with the corresponding passenger-miles. The fourth column shows the resulting number of passengers killed each year per 100 million passenger-miles; this figure is generally used as the standard yardstick of the safety achieved each year. The table indicates a steady improvement, marred by one or two bad years, particularly 1966 which started off with several similar accidents involving one particular type of aircraft. For the last five years the rate has dipped below the figure

TABLE I

ACCIDENTS WITH PASSENGER FATALITIES ON SCHEDULE AIR SERVICES 1950–1966

Year	Accidents in which passenger were killed		Fatality rate per 100 million passenger miles	Fatal accidents per 100 million miles	Fatal accidents per 100,000 aircraft hours
	Number of accidents on pass.-carrying aircraft	Number of passengers killed			
1950	27	551	3.15	3.02	0.54
1951	20	443	2.01	1.99	0.36
1952	21	386	1.54	1.90	0.35
1953	28	356	1.25	2.32	0.43
1954	28	447	1.38	2.19	0.42
1955	26	407	1.07	1.82	0.36
1956	27	552	1.25	1.71	0.34
1957	31	507	1.00	1.76	0.36
1958	30	615	1.16	1.65	0.34
1959	28	611	1.02	1.46	0.31
1960	32	847	1.25	1.66	0.37
1961	25	805	1.11	1.29	0.32
1962	28	765	0.95	1.39	0.36
1963	30	717	0.78	1.41	0.38
1964	24	658	0.62	1.05	0.29
1965	24	684	0.56	0.94	0.27
1966	24	908	0.64	0.88	0.26

of one passenger killed for each 100 million passenger-miles.

This yardstick can be used to compare the relative safety of air travel with other means of transport, such as railways or driving. In the United States over the five-year period 1960–64, it was about 0.4 for U.S. scheduled domestic airlines compared with 0.1 for railway travel and 2.2 for the highways. On the basis of "passenger-miles", flying was thus four times safer than driving.

Still another means of measuring safety is pilot fatality rates. During the earliest years of commercial airline operation, from 1920 to 1926, one in every four pilots was killed annually. By 1932 the rate had fallen to one in fifty. By 1945 it was one in five hundred and fifty. Five years later the figure was one in over seven hundred. In 1957, a record air safety year, the rate dropped to one in 5,700, and for the past few years the rate has been about one in three thousand.

These professional methods of assessing the safety of air travel are sometimes considered unsatisfactory to the travelling passenger directly concerned. A passenger is really only interested in reaching his destination safe and sound, whether it is a short flight involving only one take-off and landing, or a long distance flight involving intermediate stops with the added hazards of additional take-offs and landings and more flying hours. Working on 1966 figures, statisticians estimated that a passenger's chance of safe arrival at the end of a given flight was about 200,000 to 1. The equivalent figure for a train journey in Britain was 291,000,000 to 1.

With reference to the "pilot fatality" yardstick, it has been estimated that the average commercial pilot would have to fly for 1,000 years before becoming involved in a fatal accident. On this basis, a passenger who flies one-tenth as much as a pilot (and that represents a lot of flying for a passenger) will be 10,000 years old before he is statistically likely to be involved in an accident. A passenger is thus almost immortal!

Safety statistics indicate that for the year 1963 a passenger travelling by air in a scheduled airliner in the United States could expect to fly 435,468,000 miles before being fatally injured. This is equal to flying round the world 25,615 times and, cruising at top speed in a jet airliner, would require non-stop flying for nearly 80 years.

Statistics also show that sixteen times as many persons died after accidentally swallowing poison in 1963 as died in United States scheduled airline accidents, 18 times as many died in gun accidents, 53 times as many drowned, 67 times as many died in fires, 163 times as many died in falls and 360 times as many died in highway accidents.

Altogether, about 80,000 Americans die accidentally each year while performing presumably safe activities such as taking a bath, riding in motor-cars, working around homes and farms or getting on bicycles. Among those 80,000 unfortunate persons are a considerable proportion who insisted that aircraft flight was dangerous. Comparing the figures, in 1964 one inhabitant of the United States out of 2,400 died in accidents not connected with flying, (80,000 killed out of a population of 190,000,000), but only one out of

405,000 air travellers was killed in an aircraft accident (200 killed out of 81,000,000 air travellers).

An indication of the relative safety, or danger, of flying is provided by the insurance underwriters. These are hard-headed business men, who are outside the industry and have no axe to grind. They pay in hard cash for failures in commercial flying. The insurance companies do not bet on unknown quantities; they follow laws of probability as rigidly as the earth follows the laws of gravity. A survey of the insurance rates over the years reveals that in 1935, pilots had to pay an average extra premium of £25 for each £1000 of cover. In 1945 the extra premium was £10; in 1956 it was £3. Today, most pilots flying on world-wide scheduled flights do not have to pay any additional premium. The danger to a pilot, the one person most exposed to the hazards of flying according to the insurance assessors, is considered well within the normal risk of living. He can secure life insurance at the same low rate as an assistant in a department store, a piano tuner, a bank cashier or any other person whose daily exposure to danger approximates that of a bridge-player or a librarian. All pay the standard premiums. Among those who are charged extra premiums are dock workers, lumber-jacks, bar-tenders and jockeys.

A passenger flying fewer hours a year than an airline pilot is correspondingly less exposed to the dangers of flying. Insurance for an average flight can be purchased at odds of up to 40,000 to 1, which includes profits made by the insurance companies, the relatively high cost of selling air insurance and all other overheads.

By now you, the reader, are probably thoroughly bemused, and no nearer knowing how safe air travel is than you were when you started reading this chapter. You may feel like the salesman who, growing nervous about travelling by air, went to see his Company's statistician. "Can you tell me," he asked, "what the odds would be against my boarding an aircraft on which somebody had hidden a bomb?"

"I can't tell you until I've analysed the available data," the statistician replied. "Come back again in a week."

"Well," the salesman asked on his return, "do you know the answer?"

"Yes," the statistician said. "The odds are a million to one against your getting on an aircraft with a bomb on it."

"Those are good odds," the salesman commented. "But I'm not sure they're good enough for me. As you know, I travel a good deal."

"Well, if you want to be really safe," the statistician said, "carry a bomb with you. The odds are a thousand million to one against your boarding an aircraft with two bombs on it."

However, the short, unstatistical answer to the question posed in this chapter is undoubtedly that air travel is pretty safe. If you are an ordinary passenger making the odd business trip or flying away for your holiday, you are unlikely to end your days in an air accident. This does not mean, however, that aircraft manufacturers or airline operators are satisfied. On the contrary, continuous efforts are being made to improve still further the already high standard of safety.

The remaining chapters of this book are devoted to explaining how the present level of air safety was achieved, and to describing some of the means by which air travel is being made even safer.

2

Your safety is their concern

The four-engined Douglas DC-7 airliner accelerated down the runway. Suddenly, the aircraft struck a barrier which ripped off its landing gear and propellers. Seconds later it struck a second barrier and, with flames streaming from a blazing inboard engine, it left the runway, skidding into a small hill and shedding its wings in the process. As the plane jumped the hill, its fuselage cracked across the middle. Then, in a flurry of flames, debris and dust, the stricken aircraft ploughed across a second hill, finally coming to rest on its belly on the downslope.

Nobody, however, was killed. Nobody was even hurt, for the airliner was empty. It was crashed on purpose, as part of an elaborately staged series of experiments carried out in Arizona, U.S.A. A few months later, a surplus Lockheed Constellation suffered the same fate.

The purpose of the tests was to obtain precise information on just what happens when a large transport-type aircraft crashes. The tests provided useful information on matters such as fuel tank rupture and fuel spillage, cargo and occupant restraint and other factors related to passenger survival during a crash. The tests were conducted by the Flight Safety Foundation for the Federal Aviation Agency. These are two of the many agencies, government departments, committees, associations and other organizations concerned with safety in the air.

In the United States, air safety is looked after at government level by two agencies, the Civil Aeronautics Board and the Federal Aviation Agency. The Civil Aeronautics Board (CAB), a relatively small independent agency of the Federal Government, was established in 1938, with economic, regulatory and rule-making responsibilities. As part of the U.S. Department of Transportation, the CAB is responsible for regulating the general economics of all commercial aviation in the country, for certifying new air routes, for approving rates and fares, for supervising the financial and business competition between the airlines and, through its Bureau of Safety section, for investigating accidents. It assists the State Department in negotiations with foreign governments for the furtherance of international air transport. In addition, until 1958, the Board drafted the safety regulations and standards for licensing pilots, flight engineers, stewardesses and ground engineers, and almost everybody else having anything to do with safety in the air. In 1958, this function was transferred to the newly established Federal Aviation Agency (FAA) which absorbed its predecessor organization, the Civil Aeronautics Administration.

The FAA's responsibilities regarding the safety of aircraft begin in the design offices where aircraft are conceived and on the shop floors where they are made,

226010

and continue with the men who despatch the aircraft
at airports, the pilots who fly them, the mechanics
who maintain them, the ground specialists who control them in flight. Other FAA responsibilities include
navigation aids, the airways systems, the airports and,
significantly, research devoted to helping American
civil aviation maintain its dominant position. Approximately one-third of FAA's personnel are directly engaged in providing air traffic control services to the
thousands of aircraft operating daily, their main task
being that of keeping aircraft safely separated from
each other.

Before proceeding with a new design, aircraft manufacturers bring their project drawings and specifica-
tions to the FAA for approval, to ensure from the
outset the granting of a Type Certificate and an
Airworthiness Certificate. For example, it is important
that the size and location of the emergency exits con-
form to the requirements based on passenger seating
capacity. FAA engineers work with those of the aircraft
manufacturer throughout the entire design and manu-
facturing processes. Stress and aerodynamic calculations are cross-checked, and the aircraft itself is
checked for quality of workmanship and accuracy.
The same watchfulness is exercised over the design
and manufacture of the engines and accessories.

When the first of a new type of aircraft is produced,
it must be thoroughly tested on the ground. Aircraft
may be actually destroyed in the process of gather-
ing data on structural strength and safety. Finally,
when the ground performance measures up to standards, the aircraft gets its first FAA approval – an
Experimental Certificate of Airworthiness. It is

now ready for airborne tests and its Type Certificate.

Because of the exacting nature of the airborne tests, sometimes as many as four or five aircraft are used simultaneously to confirm and evaluate different features, such as design loads, performance, flight characteristics and the mechanical systems under actual operating conditions. Flights are made during which the aircraft is subjected to loads greater than those which will be experienced normally. Finally, the aircraft is flown on route-proving trials which simulate conditions in airline service.

When the programme has been successfully completed, a Type Certificate and a Production Certificate are issued. The Type Certificate confirms that the aircraft has met the FAA standards of construction and performance, and the Production Certificate attests the quality control of the manufacturer's production facilities. Each subsequent aircraft that conforms to the Type Certificate also gets an Airworthiness Certificate, a formal acknowledgement that it duplicates the design features and flight characteristics of the aircraft on which the Type Certificate was awarded. The Airworthiness Certificate also confirms that the aircraft is safe for commercial service.

Ensuring the safety of an aircraft does not end with an Airworthiness Certificate. Once an aircraft starts flying, the FAA is concerned with its operational safety – who is qualified to do maintenance work, and where and how it is done. The FAA controls U.S. airline maintenance programmes, setting the standards for periodic inspections and overhauls of the various aircraft components, such as the engines, instruments, and hydraulic and communications equipment. If an unsafe condition develops after the aircraft is in commercial service, the FAA notifies all operators of that particular type of aircraft or component of the corrective action they must take.

The FAA also keeps watch on the physical fitness and proficiency of pilots. All pilots must, of course, be free of medical complaints which could incapacitate them suddenly while in flight or which could prevent them from flying an aircraft safely under all conditions, and the FAA has designated more than 5,000 doctors as Aviation Medical Examiners to conduct periodic physical examinations. The proficiency of airline pilots is checked periodically by FAA inspectors, who fly with the airlines, occupying a seat in the flight compartment to observe flight techniques and procedures.

The FAA is also responsible for the overall efficiency of the complex navigational aids in use in the United States. Because of interference from other electronic devices and the nature of the atmosphere, radio signals may be accurate at ground level but inaccurate at higher levels. The FAA monitors the accuracy of the aids with its own fleet of specially instrumented aircraft. In addition to checking radio ranges, these aircraft are used to check radar tracking equipment, instrument landing systems, direction finders, marker beacons, communications between aircraft, air route traffic control centres, flight service stations (small airfields) and control towers. They are also used to test new airway aids before they are commissioned and made available for public use. The FAA's flight inspection activities extend overseas and on occasion to civil facilities in foreign countries.

International aviation relations are maintained by FAA with the International Civil Aviation Organization (ICAO) and directly with member nations. International standards, practices and safety procedures are formulated through ICAO so that pilots everywhere in the world operate under the same international rules.

One little-known FAA activity, carried out in cooperation with the State Department's Agency for International Development, is the sending of Civil Aviation Assistance Groups abroad to provide technical aid to other countries. Currently, some thirty of these groups are overseas acting as consultants on matters of aviation development and safety.

However, in spite of the far-ranging activities of the FAA in this sphere, the topic of air safety brings one name above all to mind: the Flight Safety Foundation of New York. Established in 1945, it is an independent, non-profitmaking organization dedicated solely to improving safety in aviation. The Foundation is supported by aircraft manufacturers, airline and business aircraft operators, insurance, fuel, and oil companies and banking institutions. One must credit the aviation industry with an enormous conscience for this magnanimity, because it is frequently the object of severe criticism by the Foundation.

When the Foundation started operations, safety was a dirty word in aviation circles, to be mentioned only in whispers. Airline operators felt that discussion of safety would arouse fears and thus harm sales. One of the major achievements of the Foundation is that it has helped to make "safety" respectable. It is now openly discussed; the "Welcome Aboard" pamphlet

issued by one airline to its passengers mentions the
word safety no less than eleven times.

Over the years, the Foundation has played a prin-
cipal part in safety matters ranging from the reduction
of human error in aircraft design and operation to
the promotion of crash rescue beacon development,
from crash-fire inerting system research to possible
solutions to the problem of birds on airports. It
has also conducted an extensive and spectacular
programme of wrecking aircraft, of which one was
the DC-7 crash described at the beginning of this
chapter, and illustrated on page 32.

The Foundation is principally concerned with
operating problems. It disseminates important safety
knowledge by means of several publications, with a
total print exceeding a million a year. One of the best
known is the *Aviation Mechanics Bulletin* which has
achieved ever-increasing acceptance since its inception
in 1952.

Each year the Foundation functions as a safety
catalyst by conducting an Air Safety Seminar, the
purposes of which are to provide an atmosphere of
calm objectivity away from the daily stress of critical
decision-making, to bring together professional people
with kindred interests who might not otherwise have
the opportunity to exchange ideas, and to afford an
opportunity to gain perspective. At the seminars,
design engineers obtain an appreciation of operating
problems and operators gain a better understanding
of problems that confront the engineer.

Also concerned with safety and working closely with
the Foundation is the Daniel and Florence Guggenheim Aviation Center at Cornell University, estab-

lished by the Guggenheim Foundation in 1950 to foster the improvement in aviation safety through research, education, training, and to supply air safety information to industry and to the general public. Its ultimate aim is to make flying the safest, as well as the fastest, form of transportation. The main work of the Center is to ensure the exchange of information on the applied research in the field of aviation safety. An annual *Survey of research projects in the field of aviation safety* is distributed to aviation organizations throughout the world, such as research institutes and laboratories, universities, civil aviation administrations, airlines, aircraft manufacturers, and institutes of aviation medicine.

Although the Center's objective parallels that of the Flight Safety Foundation, it does not duplicate its work. The Center is primarily concerned with research and education, whereas the Foundation is mainly involved in operating problems.

In Britain, the overall safety of air transport is the responsibility of the Air Safety and General Division of the Board of Trade, Department of Civil Aviation. The Division is divided into three sections: the Aviation Safety Directorate, the Flight Safety Directorate, and the Aviation Charters and General Branch. Two other bodies which work closely with the Air Safety Division are the Accidents Investigation Branch and the Air Registration Board. All three bodies can call upon the Royal Aircraft Establishment and other Government research establishments to aid them in any particular task.

The Directorate of Aviation Safety is concerned with licensing standards and the licensing of aircrew.

A sub-division of the Directorate is the Flight Operations Inspectorate, which was established in 1961 as a result of legislation which requires that anyone who wants to use aircraft weighing more than 5,000 pounds for the purpose of carrying paying passengers must first obtain an Air Operator's Certificate. To do this the operator has to satisfy the Director that he and his company have the required experience and technical organization and the necessary qualified staff to be a safe and competent concern. The Inspectorate checks the adequacy of the company's Operations Manual (used by pilots when flying the aeroplane), flight and landing procedures, ground bases and training procedures. The Air Registration Board assists the Inspectorate on engineering standards. The Inspectorate's work is greatly enhanced by its pilots, who are all qualified on the types of aircraft with which they deal, and who make frequent flights on the routes concerned, as well as visiting the company bases and offices.

The second Directorate, that of Flight Safety, was formed in 1961; it is the body which actually issues certificates of airworthiness upon the recommendations of the Air Registration Board, and which approves the Board's Flight Manuals from the operational safety viewpoint. Its work encompasses two main fields, one concerned with the legal requirements for things such as aircraft performance, instrumentation and safety equipment, and the other concerned with seeing how far safety can be improved by an intensive study of accident reports and records.

Work in the first field does not cover airworthiness,

Three stages in the deliberate crash of a DC-7 during a FAA test programme on crashworthiness. (*Associated Press*)

Spectacular mid-air break-up of a Vulcan bomber. (*Royal Aircraft Establishment*)

CAB accident investigator at work on a typical mass of shattered wreckage.

but deals with scales of instrumentation and the safety equipment to be carried, emergency facilities and aircrew flight time limitations. These matters may appear quite trivial, but they often entail a great deal of expensive research, and the recommendations often require airlines to spend large sums of money. For example, on the question of crash or flight data recorders, the Directorate conducted studies to find out the number of serious accidents in which, without a flight recorder, the cause would not have been established for some time, if at all. It also studied the most important information needed to be recorded for this purpose.

The objectives of the second part of the Directorate in its accident studies are to see what lessons can be learnt and what information on preventive action can be extracted and circulated to interested parties, to find out if research is needed in particular fields and if necessary to get it going, and to see if any trends in accidents can be detected and action taken before they have developed further. The Directorate concentrates on the records of British accidents, but it also uses accident records from all over the Western world. In this it is helped by the friendly relationships established with similar bodies interested in flight safety in other countries, especially the United States and Australia.

Work relating to the certification of aircraft and standards of airworthiness is delegated by the Board of Trade to the Air Registration Board. The Board is a technically and financially independent body, and its technical decisions are in no way dictated by governmental policy. Like the FAA, the Board is mainly

B

concerned with examining the design and airworthiness
of new civil aircraft, as well as surveying aircraft
regularly in relation to the renewal of their Certificates
of Airworthiness, examining licensed aircraft engineers, and publishing technical information and
airworthiness requirements. Publications issued by the
Board include the *Civil Aircraft Inspection Procedures*,
circulated in large numbers to over ninety countries,
and the internationally respected *British Civil Airworthiness Requirements*. The latter publication lays
down the minimum requirements for the strength of
the structure of British aircraft, and ensures that the
powerplant, instruments and equipment are reliable.
The requirements also ensure that aircraft are suitably
equipped to deal with emergencies, and that they have
satisfactory handling and performance qualities in
flight. The Board's Flight Test Team submits every
new aircraft to a comprehensive series of tests to
establish its airworthiness in every particular aspect;
these include a check of performance in many con-
figurations and complete handling trials both in
normal flight and in various conditions of emergency.
The Flight Team tests all aircraft, ranging from light
types such as the Beagle Terrier, to large airliners
such as the VC-10. In addition, foreign aircraft
purchased by British operators are tested. The Team's
technical competence is such that its suggestions are
heeded even when the aircraft comes from an experienced and respected manufacturer such as Boeing.
When BOAC purchased its fleet of 707s, the Board
insisted that the fin area be increased to ease the
pilot's task of controlling the big aircraft during certain "engine-out" emergency conditions. Boeing

publicly acknowledged the advice of the Board and, in addition to modifying the BOAC aircraft, supplied parts to other operators so that they could modify their fleets.

The Board also ensures that every British aircraft is backed up by a comprehensive range of technical publications covering operation, maintenance and overhaul. These manuals are compiled and certified by persons approved by the Board. Once a British operator has taken delivery of an aircraft, he must plan its maintenance in accordance with the conditions under which it will be operating. The maintenance schedules are examined and approved by the Board, and must be related to the routes over which the aircraft will fly. The Board itself issues the previously mentioned *Flight Manual*, which contains basic details of the aircraft's performance under all conditions, its limitations and operating procedures.

Many other organizations are concerned wholly or in part with increased safety in the air. Not the least of these is the Flight Safety Committee, roughly Britain's equivalent of the Daniel and Florence Guggenheim Aviation Center in the United States. The Committee came into being in 1959, when concern was expressed regarding the air safety record in Britain compared with other countries. The Committee collects safety information and re-transmits it to airline managements and people operating ground services; it also stimulates and organizes discussion of remedial and preventive measures. The committee's messages are conveyed by its magazine FOCUS, which comes out six times a year, by the Flight Safety Discussion Group, and by the showing of Flight Safety films. Currently the committee has organized an accident-information exchange scheme in which eighteen British airlines are participating.

Aircrew have a special responsibility regarding safety in the air, and the subject naturally plays an important part in the aims and activities of the various pilot and aircrew associations. In the United States, the powerful Airline Pilots Association holds an annual Air Safety Forum. In Britain, the equivalent British Air Line Pilots Association, although concerned primarily with the immediate problems of pilots, has the motto *Service with Safety* which underlines its main aim. In 1947 an Air Safety and Technical Committee was formed to look at these two aspects of the pilots' job, and in 1962, due to the amount of work involved, a separate sub-group of the Technical Committee was formed, known as the Accident Investigation Group. This now meets at regular intervals to discuss air safety matters and also to consider reports of accidents. When an accident occurs to a British aircraft, a three-man team of the AIG is formed to enquire into the circumstances and to make recommendations. This team is purely a technical team and does not interest itself in industrial matters; it is therefore able to establish close co-operation with the Accident Investigation Branch of the Board of Trade, and also with the appropriate operator.

The longer established Guild of Air Pilots and Air Navigators, concerned primarily with legislative matters, also devotes much of its energies towards the promotion of greater safety, particularly the examination of pilots who aspire to instruct. The Guild is not afraid to speak out if it feels that safety may be compromised. Thus, when the subject of noise near airports was in the public mind, the Guild stressed that any lessening of noise for those on the ground should not be achieved at the expense of increased danger for those in the air; it stated that pilots must not be expected to tax their skill or the performance of their aircraft merely to reduce noise by a few decibels.

An indication of the extensive interest of the Guild in air safety was given in a paper in 1963 expressing concern at the serious deficiencies in the provision of terminal aids throughout the world. The paper pointed out that the need for precision flying and navigation, especially during approach and landing, constituted the most exacting demand of modern civil aircraft operation, yet many international airports did not provide essential navigation aids. The Guild pointed out that it was not merely a matter of radio and radar aids; in many cases visual aids to approach and landing were poor, while the state of en-route navigational aids was far from satisfactory. Navigational aids had not, in fact, kept pace with the rapid technical advances in aircraft design and operation. The Guild, by virtue of its non-partisan constitution and the experience of its members, thus made a practical contribution in the vital matter of international air safety. To enable the Guild to continue and expand its efforts to improve safety in the air, its constitution was revised in 1964 to form a charitable fund so that it could receive monetary donations from Trusts.

Lack of space prevents mention of the many other government departments, societies, committees and groups in many other countries. However, whatever their names, and whatever their country, they all have a common bond – your safety is their concern.

3

Investigating an accident

"Airliner crashes in valley. Many dead." Such headlines in a newspaper or on the evening's television newscast are all that the average person hears of an aircraft accident.

Behind the public's view, however, a great deal of activity takes place, for an accident involving casualties or serious or unaccountable damage initiates a train of events unparallelled in any other form of public transport. All such accidents are the subject of an official investigation, undertaken by the Accident Investigation Branch in Britain, and the Civil Aeronautics Board in the United States. Other interested bodies are, of course, the airline operator, the manufacturer of the aircraft concerned, and, occasionally, the local air traffic control organization.

It is vital that the cause of an accident be determined in order to prevent a similar accident occurring. Basically, the investigation of an accident, like that of a crime, is a problem in detection, calling for observation and deduction, and sometimes for scientific experiments to test a suggested explanation or theory. Aircraft accident investigation involves technical skill of the highest order, based upon a background of engineering science and aeronautical experience.

The photograph on page 33 of the scrapyard-like remains of an accident gives a good idea of the tangled mass of metal and wire from which the accident investigator starts to gather his clues. It seems impossible, looking at such a jumbled muddle of wreckage, that a true explanation of what went wrong could ever be discovered. Transforming the debris into items for examination is a long job and helps to explain why solutions to air accidents are rarely forthcoming in the days immediately following the event.

As soon as an accident is reported, an investigator visits the scene of the crash. Most of the damage is usually caused when the aircraft hits the ground, and the investigator, therefore, must try to isolate the impact damage from any damage that may have been sustained while the aircraft was in the air.

In cases where the aircraft breaks up in the air, the arrangement of the remains on the ground, known as the wreckage trail, is of vital importance. While the wreckage is on the ground the location of all the major portions is plotted accurately on a map. This plan of the wreckage then gives clues to the sequence in which failure occurred in the air. It is not just a matter of assuming that the piece of wreckage furthest down the line was the first to have broken away. The pattern is complicated by the fact that the momentum of heavy components, such as an engine or under-carriage leg, tends to carry them further than light items, like pieces of fuselage skin which, offering more resistance, tend to flutter almost straight down. The pattern may be further complicated by high winds. However, years of study and experience now enable trained investigators to estimate the rate at which wreckage of different weights and shapes descend.

Wreckage trails vary enormously, ranging from a few feet to hundreds of miles in length. The complete absence of a wreckage trail presents a special case, for it implies that the aircraft was intact at the moment of impact. In such cases, however, the investigators have to be very careful to ensure that the aircraft wreckage is, in fact, complete, for a single missing piece could be of vital importance.

One of the most remarkable attempts to obtain a wreckage trail occurred during the salvage of the remains of a prototype Victor 2 bomber which crashed in the Irish Sea in 1959, twenty-five miles from land. Three-quarters of the aircraft was salvaged in eight months, and during recovery operations investigators mapped the location of major pieces on the sea bottom. A considerable degree of success was attained, and it was established that certain parts of the aircraft had broken away before the final impact with the sea. The wreckage trail also indicated that the crew had made preparations to escape; this information proved to be crucial in the successful investigation which followed the accident.

These notes on the value of wreckage trails in the investigation of an accident indicate the importance of preventing the ordinary public from moving any piece of wreckage they might find after an accident. The location of such items should be pointed out to official investigators. Even worse than the disturbance of wreckage is the collection of "souvenirs", which could remove a part containing a vital clue to the cause of an accident.

After the required information has been obtained at the site of a crash, the wreckage is transported to the building being used for the investigation. Every piece is studied for clues as to its identity. Such things as type of construction, material, paint colours and part numbers assist at this stage. Pieces can sometimes be identified by matching their broken edges with those of another, identified, piece. As the parts are identified, the aircraft is reconstructed. A typical result, resembling a garish three-dimensional jig-saw puzzle, is shown in the photograph on page 64. The jig-saw reconstruction serves a number of purposes. A missing piece is readily apparent, and the common boundaries of adjacent pieces are available for later study.

The analysis of the reconstruction is a highly specialized task. Every fact, however small, must be discovered and carefully considered. There is no set procedure for the examination of wreckage as this differs from crash to crash, and experienced investigators tend to develop approaches of their own. Whatever technique is used, the aim is to find the answers to the four basic questions of "what happened", "where", "when" and "how", which will lead to the all-important answer to the question "why?"

Somewhere, the wreckage contains evidence which will lead to the discovery of the cause of the accident; it will either contain the technical feature itself, or it will contain nothing. The latter situation indicates that the answer is not to be found on the aircraft, but elsewhere, thus giving a lead to the next line to take in the search. Initially, the investigator will probably just look at the facts in the wreckage itself, examining the breakages, the distortion, the scratch, the tear and the burnt and unburnt portions. These features will resolve themselves as local events and sequences and will ultimately add up to a picture of the actual events that took place. At this stage, the investigator does not look *for* any particular information; if he does, there is a danger that he will only see damage associated with one particular line of thought, and other vital information will be missed.

After the general survey, the wreckage is examined closely, piece by piece, and all the facts noted. It is often convenient to use copies of the aircraft constructors' engineering drawings for this purpose, but perspective sketches may be prepared and photographs utilized.

Any blackening and discolouration due to fire is of prime interest. Fire is, of course, the great enemy of the accident investigator, as it can destroy valuable clues, especially if it breaks out after impact with the ground. However, investigators can determine whether it started in the air before or after breakage, or whether it occurred after impact with the ground. Evidence of fire helps to determine the sequence of any disintegration. For example, if one piece of structure is found blackened with smoke, while another, originally joined to it, is completely clean, this is evidence that the two pieces broke apart before the fire had time to reach them. Fire damage can also provide clues to the settings of movable surfaces, such as the elevators, rudder and their trim tabs.

Minor scratches and indentations are also of interest

to investigators, especially in accidents involving structural disintegration in the air. A scratch on one piece ending abruptly at a fracture indicates that the two pieces had separated before the scratch was caused. If a scratch extends across a fracture, it must have been made while the two pieces were joined.

One of the most important clues provided by scratch or impact marks is when pieces of the front of the fuselage or the wing strike the tailplane. When an aircraft disintegrates in the air, the first consideration is to discover which broke off first, the wings or the tailplane. Eye-witnesses are rarely of help, as the one follows the other so closely as to appear instantaneous. In fact, on the fortuitous occasions when the disintegration of an aircraft has been recorded on film, even the cine camera has not been fast enough to record the complete sequence of failure. In more than one accident, a piece has fractured in the split second while the film was moving from one exposure to the next. In these examples, the answer to the accidents lay in the wreckage. Scratch marks, left by pieces of the front of the fuselage or wing striking the tailplane, normally indicate that the tailplane was still in position when the wing failed. (See photograph, page 128.)

During the investigation of one accident with which the author was associated, traces of red glass were found inside the shattered navigation lamp housing in the left-hand wing tip. The slivers of glass were identified as coming from the right-hand wing tip navigation lamp, showing that somehow the two wing tips had struck each other. Other evidence indicated that the tail unit had broken away, causing the nose of the aircraft to pitch down sharply. The wings, presented broadside on to the full force of the airstream, failed and folded right back until the tips touched!

On another occasion a piece of carpet was lodged inside the fractured stub of a tailplane. The aircraft concerned had broken up in the air, and investigators suspected that the tailplane might have broken away first. There was evidence, however, that the tailplane had been struck in flight and there were unusual blue paint smears around the fracture line. The smears were present on both the piece that had broken away and on the section remaining on the aircraft. Close examination of the smears indicated that the paint had been applied from front to rear. This piece of evidence suggested that the tailplane had been knocked off. The question was, by what?

The investigators searched for blue-coloured components and found several, including the cabin seats and the external decoration of the aircraft. The paint smears on the tail were analysed by chemists and found that it was the same as that on the seats. The carpeting gave the vital clue, for it was jammed into the broken stub of the tailplane in such a way that it could only have lodged there during the actual breaking of the tailplane.

What did all this mean to the investigators? They deduced that the tailplane must have been in a position to be struck from forward by items from the fuselage and, more important, that the fuselage itself must have been substantially intact to be supporting the tail. As the tailplane had been struck by items from within the main cabin, it was deduced that the fuselage had failed locally in this area. Further examination confirmed that this was, indeed, what had happened.

The external examination of the jig-saw is primarily concerned with structural features. The type of failure between sections is important – whether the fracture was due to tension, compression or to fatigue – as it indicates the direction in which the pieces failed. This is readily discernible to the trained investigator by a study of the torn edges. The direction of failure can also be determined by microscopic examination of the paint, which leaves a characteristic saw-tooth pattern on metal sheet that has been torn apart.

The attention given to the structural damage during an investigation does not imply that a structural failure is always a prime suspect. In practice, the number of accidents due to structural failure is a small proportion of the total. This part of an investigation, however, indicates the overall sequences of structural disintegration, and sometimes provides the clues from which the primary cause of the accident is determined.

The systems and their instruments provide different kinds of clues, which are discovered through a different approach. This part of an accident investigation requires, perhaps, an even greater diversity of knowledge than is required for structural investigations, because of the great variety of scientific principles embodied in mechanical and electrical components.

As in the case of the structure, damaged instruments are carefully examined for general clues without necessarily being suspected of causing the accident.

When examining a system, the investigator first determines the basic power requirements for the operation of the system – its electrical and hydraulic needs. He then finds out if this power was being supplied when the accident occurred, for there would be no point in trying to find out how components were behaving if they were not being supplied with power.

The generation of electrical and hydraulic power involves the use of rotating mechanisms and the investigator determines whether these were running at the moment of impact. In this instance the final impact which all too often destroys evidence may also create evidence, because there is usually a marked difference between a component damaged by impact alone and one damaged by the combined effect of impact and its own movement. The impact with the ground may also lock some slow moving components, such as the screwjacks used to operate a wing leading edge-slat, or trailing edge flap. This enables the investigator to determine whether the state of operation was normal or abnormal.

The shattered remains of radio valves and lamp bulbs can also supply valuable evidence. The filament in a valve consists of an extremely fine tungsten wire which is heated when operated. The filament is normally working in a vacuum and therefore never oxidizes. However, if the glass shatters when the filament is hot, oxidization takes place, dissolving the filament. Thus, if an investigator finds a discoloured filament, he knows that the valve was on when it fractured. If a valve is switched off the filament cools extremely rapidly, so that unless a valve was actually on at the moment the glass failed, the filament will always be free from oxidization.

Examination of the filaments of the small lamps of

the type used for warning indicators and panel lighting can also indicate whether these were lit at the
moment of impact. If the lamp is on, the filament is
hot and it tends to distort if shock loaded; if the lamp
is off, the filament is cold and does not distort. Distortion can be detected even if the filament itself
separates.

The study of the lamp filaments that survive an
accident is important, as lamps are used to indicate
faults in systems, a group of lamps often being mounted
on a small "central warning" panel in front of the
pilot. If a system fails the appropriate warning lamp
lights; the pilot then identifies the failure from a code
on the panel and takes the appropriate action. Examination of such lamps after a crash will indicate
whether they were on or off at the moment of impact.
A warning lamp which was on gives the investigator a
ready clue of a possible cause of the accident. However, the search for other clues does not cease if such
a warning lamp is found to have been on; unless all
the facts are studied, a wrong answer might be
assumed.

The flying control runs, those of the ailerons, rudder
and elevator, receive special study during an accident
investigation. First they are examined for continuity
by checking the individual rods, cables and levers
making up the circuit. This sounds simple enough, but
impact damage may stretch the investigator's skill to
the limit. If a failure in a system matches damage on
the surrounding structure, the investigator assumes
that the circuit at that point was intact at the moment
of impact. If the circuit has failed in isolation, this
could mean that it failed in flight. Other evidence of

pre-impact failure is provided by discrepancies between the setting of the pilot's controls and the position
of the relevant control surfaces.

Investigators sometimes call for special experiments
to help prove the soundness of a particular line of
reasoning. If evidence points to a structural weakness
in a certain part, a strength test can be carried out on a
replica in the laboratory. To check a suspected aerodynamic fault, test flights using another aircraft of the
same type are sometimes made. Flights of this nature
were made during the investigation into the Lockheed
Electra of Northwest Airlines which, on March 17,
1960, disintegrated over Tell City, Indiana, killing
all sixty-three people on board. At least one wing had
failed in flight, and the accident bore a startling resem-
blance to an earlier Electra crash at Buffalo, Texas,
which was still under investigation.

As previously mentioned, structural failures are
rare, and the accident shook the industry, especially as
the Electra had been particularly thoroughly tested.
The new airliner had been warmly praised by the airlines from every standpoint, including that of safety.

Working with the CAB, the FAA ordered the manufacturer to put the Electra through a series of extensive tests. Lockheed took a brand-new aircraft off the
production line and carefully instrumented it so that
forces imposed by turbulence on the structure and
powerplants could be measured in flight. Test pilots
then flew the aircraft into a mountainous area in
California notorious for its severe gust conditions. For
weeks on end they flew the aircraft into the treacherous
air currents at varying speeds and varying weights,
while the various stresses were recorded and analysed.

On the ground a second aircraft was subjected to a series of static tests, many of which duplicated those the aircraft had already been through as part of its certification programme. The tests checked the wing deflection rates and structural stiffness, and whether abnormal stresses and vibration could lead to metal fatigue. In addition a wing was deliberately destroyed in a series of progressively severe static tests. No effort was spared to find the answer to the mysterious failure. Work was conducted in three shifts a day, seven days a week. Computers were diverted from their current work to help analyse the flight test data. Some engineers worked as many as ninety hours a week.

The solution was found within two months. Studying the streams of data obtained during the hazardous test flights and during the thousands of laboratory tests, the investigators' attention focused on the outboard engines and their mountings. The information indicated the following sequence of events in the two crashes.

The rapidly spinning engine, together with its propeller, acted as a huge gyroscope. If the aircraft encountered turbulence of a particular intensity the jolt could be sufficient to upset the smooth running of the engines. Disturbed, the propeller started to wobble, and its uneven motion was transmitted back to the wing, causing it to vibrate and flutter. Like the echo from a hill, the wing in turn sent additional disruptive forces back to the engine and propeller assembly, making it wobble even more. Engineers call this phenomena whirl mode, and as far as the Electra was concerned, it was uncontrolled whirl mode. The next step in the chain reaction was that the whirl mode frequency slowed down, but increased in violence. Initially, the frequency was about five cycles a second, but it was reduced to three cycles a second.

Ordinarily, the Electra would have survived this, but three cycles a second happened to be the maximum frequency at which the wing could flutter. The instant the two vibration frequencies reached the same level, extremely high forces were experienced, sufficient to fracture the engine mounting. Known as harmonic or dynamic coupling, the effect was similar to that of a high musical note breaking a glass which has the same vibration frequency.

On the Electra the elapsed time between the jolt exciting the engine and causing the whirl mode and the attaining of forces sufficient to wrench the wing off was only twenty seconds.

After the discovery of the cause came the cure to prevent similar crashes. The wing was strengthened at key structural areas, a process which added 1,400 pounds of weight and cost a total of over £8 million. In addition to advancing knowledge of harmonic coupling problems, the Electra investigation focused attention on clean air turbulence. Unlike turbulence associated with thunderstorms, clean air turbulence cannot be predicted or detected by conventional radar. To help find out more about it, a Senate Committee added £3 million to a Commerce Department appropriations measure, to be used for research into high-altitude weather.

The most famous and searching laboratory tests made in support of an accident investigation were carried out after a Comet jet liner crashed off the

Island of Elba in 1954. The complex experiments went
far beyond anything attempted previously, and the
full story of this test and its important contribution to
increased safety in the air is told in Chapter 8.

"Contributing to increased safety in the air." This
is the motive behind the determination to discover the
reason for every aircraft accident, particularly if
fatalities are involved; and, with few exceptions, aircraft accident investigations do result in increased
safety. Where the fault is a defect duplicated in other
aircraft of the same type, the defect is put right before
it can cause another accident. Where the cause is
associated with a design feature adopted on other aircraft, details of the investigation are circulated to the
manufacturers concerned.

An example of this interchange of information is
given by the "deep stall" accident suffered by the
prototype BAC One-Eleven in 1963. This sad accident
not only ensured that the One-Eleven had very good
stalling characteristics when it entered service, but it
contributed to air safety in general. The British Aircraft Corporation made the results of its investigation
known to other manufacturers both in Britain and
overseas, so that the knowledge gained would be of
lasting benefit to the general safety of aviation. The
information was of particular interest to the Douglas
Aircraft Company, who at that time were engaged
upon the design of their DC-9, an airliner very similar
to the One-Eleven, incorporating rear-mounted engines and a T-tail. As a result of the information received on the One-Eleven stall difficulties, Douglas
increased the size of the tailplane on their new aircraft and introduced a leading edge "Vortilon" to

improve the pitch-down characteristics of the wing.

If the probable cause of an accident is found to be a fault in air traffic control procedure, other control authorities are notified so that they can take action if necessary to prevent a recurrence of the mistake. In cases where the probable cause was an error on the part of the pilot, other pilots are warned of the circumstances of the mishap.

The use of the word "probable" in the previous paragraph is deliberate. For, however convinced they are that their investigators have discovered the truth, the CAB prefixes every crash solution with the word "probable". The Board never wants to close its books completely on an air tragedy, as another accident may some day shed new light on an old one.

The only notable exception to this interchange of accident information is Aeroflot, the state airline of the U.S.S.R. Aeroflot is the world's biggest airline and operates a wide variety of modern jet and turbojet airliners. The airline obtain full details of all the accident reports published in the West, but gives very little in return. The reason for this is not clear, for available evidence indicates that the airline has a safety record of which it need not be ashamed, and circulation of the causes of its accidents would undoubtedly be of interest to the West in some instances.

4

Safety in design

Safety is a prime consideration from the very earliest stage in the design of an aircraft. For example, consider the design of a large airliner. During the initial stages of development, while the general layout is being determined, a variety of wing positions, engine locations and fuselage shapes will be investigated. As far as the fuselage is concerned, two basic shapes at least will almost certainly be considered; a simple cylinder of circular cross section, and a double-bubble with two decks, as these basic sections are ideal for pressurization.

The two-deck double-bubble configuration is attractive, as it offers a stiff structure for a low weight. Two decks, however, have several disadvantages from the safety aspect. In the event of an emergency landing with the wheels up (experience shows that this happens, sooner or later, on all aircraft with retracting landing gears) it would be difficult for passengers on the upper deck to escape because of their height from the ground. In the event of a two-deck aircraft ditching in the sea, the passengers from the lower deck would have to climb stairs in order to escape from the upper deck, as the lower cabin doors and emergency exits would be below the water-line.

This last disadvantage could be overcome by mounting the engines at the rear of the fuselage and adopting a low wing. However, engines mounted at the rear introduce the possibility of the airflow over the wing causing a reduction in engine power at high angles of attack. Also, such an engine position almost always brings with it the need for a high-mounted tailplane and this in turn introduces the possibility of undesirable stall characteristics.

The merits and disadvantages of high and low wing positions are compared. A low wing results in a short, sturdy, landing gear, but increases the engine ingestion problem. A high wing eases the engine ingestion problem, but requires a stalky landing gear. It also reduces the space available for fuel as, from the safety point of view, it is undesirable to carry fuel in that portion of the wing passing over the fuselage. A high wing also has the disadvantage that the top surface cannot be inspected for snow deposits prior to take-off as readily as the top surface of a low wing.

Sometimes fundamental design changes are made in the interest of increased safety. An example of this occurred on the Concorde supersonic airliner. To reduce drag to the minimum while cruising at supersonic speeds a visor extends to fair, or streamline, the windscreen smoothly into the nose of the fuselage. Initially this was constructed of aluminium and was retracted into the nose for taking off and landing. Although great care was taken to ensure that the visor would always work, airline pilots pointed out that if somehow it became stuck in the extended position, they would have to make a landing virtually blind, as forward vision through the visor was limited to small cut-outs. Accordingly the visor was redesigned as a one-piece transparent unit, giving almost normal vision forward when it is extended. The penalty for additional safety was almost negligible as, although the transparent visor increased drag slightly at supersonic speeds this was largely offset by a reduction at subsonic speeds. The visor is shown on page 65.

Of fundamental importance is the question of the number of engines, and the relationship between the power of the engines and the airframe characteristics. The basic aim is to provide the same degree of safety irrespective of the number of engines. On long-range aircraft four engines are a logical choice, and for small aircraft operating over short stages two engines can readily provide the economy and degree of safety required. For aircraft designed to operate over medium stage lengths, around the 1000-mile mark, the choice is less easy. Considerations taken into account include whether the aircraft is likely to operate extensively over the sea or regions of mountains, and whether it is ever likely to be "stretched" into a relatively long-range aircraft which will operate over such terrain. Whatever the final choice, the airliner will have to meet strict governmental regulations of safety and airworthiness regarding fundamental flying characteristics. For example, consider the vital process of taking off. During take-off some things, such as the strength and direction of the wind, and the length and slope of the runway, will be ascertained at the time by the pilot. Other things, such as possible engine failure at a critical moment cannot be determined, and therefore the requirements specify that should this happen the pilot must be able to maintain control and continue flying safely.

The requirements also lay down minimum standards for the strength of the structure, such as that of the wings and fuselage, and for the energy to be absorbed by the landing gear. In Britain these design requirements for civil aircraft are laid down in "British Civil Airworthiness Requirements" issued by the Air Registration Board, and for military aircraft in "Design Requirements for Aircraft for the Royal Air Force and Royal Navy (AvP 970)" prepared by the Ministry of Technology (formerly the Ministry of Aviation). In the United States the comparable requirements are formulated by the Federal Aviation Agency.

These regulations have evolved through successive generations of aircraft, many of them being the result of lessons learned from past accidents. However, it must be pointed out that, strict as they are, the requirements represent a compromise between safety and economy. If safety were the only consideration in designing an airliner, the result would still not be an aeroplane that was 100 per cent safe, but it would undoubtedly be so expensive that passengers would not be able to afford to fly in it. The requirements have to strike a balance between what is required to provide the maximum safety and what is required to make an economically practicable aeroplane. Thus, to a certain extent, the requirements represent a calculated risk. For example, the requirements specify that the structure has to be capable of withstanding the loads imposed by a vertical wind gust of fifty feet per second encountered at cruising speed. More powerful wind gusts exist, of course, and in fact the requirement was framed in the knowledge that a stronger gust is likely to be encountered by an airliner about once every four million miles, equal to about two hundred trips round the world. An encounter with such a gust does not automatically mean that the aircraft will break up, for the designers build in a "factor of safety" of at least one-and-a-half to make the aircraft half as strong again as would be necessary to withstand a fifty feet per second gust. However, it is known that gusts occasionally exist of a magnitude likely to damage an aircraft. Why do not the requirements specify the strongest gust ever recorded? The answer is that the aircraft would be very much heavier, and thus carry a smaller number of passengers paying higher fares, to be prepared for an eventuality that will almost certainly never arise. Even if it was possible to design an aircraft to withstand the highest gust ever recorded, there would be no guarantee that, one day, somewhere, it would not encounter an even more powerful gust. One has to stop somewhere.

Similar compromises have to be made on virtually all aircraft. On a fighter-bomber, for example, it is desirable to provide armour protection for the pilot. The better he is protected, the greater the chance of the aircraft completing a mission. However, more armour means less gun ammunition or a reduction in bomb load. In fact, one ground attack aeroplane was built so heavily armoured that it simply could not fly. The pilot was completely protected, but the aircraft was hardly an effective fighting machine!

The point about compromise has been dealt with at

some length to make it clear that safety in aircraft design involves calculated risks, as most things do in everyday life. For example, drivers could obtain an almost crash-proof car by paying twice the normal price. But the average driver considers the expense unjustified and accepts the risk involved in driving a conventional car. People even take risks when increased safety can be purchased quite cheaply. It has been proved conclusively that the use of seat belts in motor cars significantly reduces the chance of injury and death in most serious accidents; yet the majority of motorists are not prepared to pay the relatively small sum involved. They take a calculated risk that they will not be involved in an accident and if they are, that they will survive anyway. In aircraft design, the acceptable margin of risk is much smaller, but it follows the same principle.

When the general configuration of a new aircraft has been determined, design work starts on the basic structure. The main parts of the aircraft, such as the wing, fuselage and landing gear, must be strong enough to withstand the loads to which they will be subjected. It is a simple matter to design a structure strong enough to withstand such loads. It is less easy to design a structure that is strong enough and as light as possible. It is even more difficult to design the lightest possible structure able to withstand loads applied repeatedly, such as those experienced when an aircraft lands and takes off, when the fuselage is pressurized, and when wind gusts are met in flight.

The repeated application of such loads causes the phenomenon known as metal fatigue: that is, the tendency of metal to fail under the repeated application of relatively low loads, although it is strong enough to withstand a higher load applied once or twice. This can be demonstrated quite simply with a paper clip; these are impossible to break by hand by pulling at the ends, and yet they can be broken easily if bent back and forth a few times. Metal fatigue has played a disastrous part in aircraft design. Structures which were strong enough initially failed in service through the repeated applications of relatively light loads.

Today the effects of fatigue are being combated in two main ways. First, better materials have been developed. Early turbojet and turboprop airliners were designed around high strength, zinc-rich, aluminium alloys but, unfortunately, high strength did not necessarily lead to long fatigue lives. Also, some of the early alloys were exceedingly "scratch conscious", necessitating great care in the design and manufacture of components in order to avoid building in fatigue points. Experience showed that often it was a small detail that led to a serious fatigue crack. Recent airliners have discarded the zinc-rich alloys in favour of copper-rich alloys. Although these have lower strength, they tend to remain crack-free or, if a crack develops, its rate of propagation is much slower.

However, the main assault against fatigue has been in design rather than in materials. One of two philosophies, known as "safe-life" and "fail-safe", are generally adopted in designing structures.

The safe-life philosophy is normally applied to parts only when it is not practicable either to duplicate or to design to fail safe, such as in the landing gear

legs, and flap and slat tracks. The structure is designed with the objective of achieving freedom from
cracks during the operational life of the aircraft;
furthermore, should a crack develop, it will propagate
slowly, so that it can be detected during normal
inspections long before it has reached dangerous
proportions.

Wherever possible, however, structures are designed to the "fail-safe" principle which is similar to
that of wearing both a belt and braces to hold up
one's trousers. Main load-carrying members, such as
wing spars, are duplicated so that if any one of them
fails, the remaining members can withstand the loads,
permitting the safe completion of a flight. The remaining structure is usually designed to withstand these
ordinary loads for a longer period than the interval
specified between major inspections of the structure.
The "double structure" is a similar fail-safe design
and simply means the use of two smaller members in
place of one large one. This type of structure is widely
used where it is imperative to arrest cracks, as in
wing spar booms. Following the experience gained
during the investigation into the Comet accidents,
described in the chapter entitled "Riddle over the
Mediterranean", pressurized fuselages are now provided with "crack stoppers". These are strips of re-
inforcing, designed to prevent a crack in the fuselage
skin from "tearing" to an extent that would cause
catastrophic failure.

On the Boeing 737 airliner the fail-safe characteristics of the fuselage are enhanced by the use of new
bonded skin doublers. These doublers are arranged in
the shape of a "waffle" grid, to box in any potential

circumferential and longitudinal cracks. The fail-safe
effectiveness of the "waffle" doublers was tested on a
specimen fuselage; pressures up to the equivalent of
flight at 40,000 feet were applied while the cabin was
pierced in numerous places with a sharp guillotine-
like probe. No serious failure resulted.

The "back-up structure" is another common fail-
safe design. This method is often incorporated in the
passenger windows on high-flying pressurized airliners, and entails the fitting of a second, inner window,
capable of withstanding the pressure loads should the
outer window fail.

The care taken in the design stages and the extensive structural testing conducted in the process of
obtaining certificates of airworthiness have made
accidents due to structural failure extremely rare.
The few that have occurred have either been caused
by violent storms or by clean-air turbulence.

The philosophy of safety is continued in the design
of the basic systems. Much useful information is
obtained by talking to operators while they are being
schemed. For example, quite drastic changes were
made in the Hawker Siddeley Trident flying control
system, and also in the nose undercarriage, as a result
of discussions with American Airlines and Air Canada.

On modern high-speed airliners the control surfaces
are powered; that is, they are moved by hydraulic
jacks and not directly by the pilot. The air loads are
too high for the surfaces to be moved manually, as
they were on piston-engined airliners and still are on
light aircraft. Once the decision to use powered controls has been taken, the supply of the necessary power
becomes vitally important. The supply must not fail,

for without it the aircraft would be uncontrollable. Power is ensured by providing duplicate jacks, with separate hydraulic pipe lines supplied from independent sources. The two jacks can be arranged so that both act on the same control surface, or so that the control surface can be divided into two or more sections, each section being operated by a separate jack.

The latter method is used on the BAC VC-10, on which each aileron and elevator is divided into two and the rudder into three sections, each actuated by its own adjacent and separately powered hydraulic jack. The safety conferred by this arrangement was dramatically demonstrated during an early test flight, when an elevator hinge bracket broke. Had a single-piece elevator been fitted, all longitudinal control would have been lost and the aircraft would almost certainly have crashed. As it was, the pilot was able to return to base safely.

On the Hawker Siddeley Trident single control surfaces are used, each powered by no less than three jacks. All three jacks are normally working all the time and are thus said to be "triplexed". This is quite different from systems in which the jacks are duplicated, or triplicated; in such systems only one jack is working at a time, and if it fails the spare, or duplicate, jack is brought into operation. The big advantage of a triplex installation is that if one system fails, the remaining systems continue to work without any action on the part of the pilot, eliminating the need for a hurried change-over from one system to another. This is clearly advantageous in automatic landings. On the Trident, if one jack fails, the two remaining jacks continue to provide full control, and if two jacks fail, the remaining jack is sufficiently powerful to ensure the completion of the flight and a safe landing.

The triplex system on the Trident was enhanced by the three-engined layout, as basic sources of hydraulic power could be independently provided by a pump on each of the three engines. Further safety was ensured by the provision of two electrically-driven stand-by pumps for use if any one of the three main pumps failed. This system is illustrated on page 81.

To provide for the extremely remote possibility of all the main and stand-by hydraulic systems failing, an air-turbine pump was installed. This consists of a small propeller-driven hydraulic pump, which drops out into the airstream automatically to supply the vital hydraulic power in the event of a complete power failure.

Many other safety features are built into hydraulically-operated systems; one example is the wheel brakes. On most airliners one hydraulic system normally pressurizes a number of hydraulic cylinders in each brake. Should this system fail, a second system can be used to operate, through separate pressure pipe lines, a second set of cylinders in the brake. Should both systems fail, hydraulic accumulators retain enough pressure to give five or six full brake applications, which is ample to enable the pilot to make a safe landing.

Another fundamental power requirement on an airliner is that of electricity, and similar steps are taken to ensure that an adequate supply will always be available. Thus on modern airliners, electrical power is provided by two, three or four generators

Three dimensional jig-saw reconstruction of the Boeing 720B lost over Miami, Florida, on February 12, 1963.

The transparent visor adopted on the Concorde supersonic airliner, (i) visor in use (ii) showing absence of visor.

mounted one on each engine. The generators provide independent sources of supply, each feeding isolated, or separate, electrical channels. Special attention is paid to safety requirements; the circuits are designed to fail safe, and the layout of the electrical installation is planned to ensure that no single fault can affect more than one electrical channel. In the extremely unlikely event of complete failure of all the generators, emergency services can be supplied from a battery.

Some aircraft carry an auxiliary power unit and in many cases these can be used in the air to provide yet another source of hydraulic and electrical power.

In addition to the attention given to the safety aspect of the basic features of an aircraft, "safety in design" is apparent in many other systems and components. For example, on all but the smallest private aircraft, dual wheels are fitted to the landing gear, so that if a tyre should burst, the adjacent tyre will prevent a violent lurch to one side or the loss of directional control in the case of the nose leg. On airliners the landing gear is usually retracted hydraulically, and in spite of the care devoted to the design of the system and intensive testing on rigs, it is not unknown for an unforeseen "gremlin" to cause the landing gear to remain up when the pilot selects "landing gear down". To overcome this problem, two separate sources of hydraulic power usually supply the landing gear jacks and, in the event of both of these failing, designers try to ensure that the gear can be unlocked so that it can fall freely under gravity, a spring strut being used to lock the legs in the "down" position. Where the landing gear configuration is such that the legs will not extend under their own weight, they can

c

be extended by emergency supplies or wound down manually.

In spite of the duplication and the care taken in detail design and in testing, one misfortune which seems to befall all aeroplanes with a retractable landing gear is the necessity of making a belly landing with the wheels up. Designers are aware of this possibility and strengthen the structure locally to minimize the damage. Sometimes very positive design steps are taken; for example, the Hawker Siddeley 125 executive jet incorporates a metal skid under the wing. In a landing with the wheels up, this skid, which is readily replaceable, abrades away and minimizes the risk of damage to the wing and fuselage structure which would be costly to repair. Another example is given by the long-range versions of the Comet. These airliners carry extra fuel in pod tanks mounted on the leading edge of the wing. In a wheels-up landing the tanks would scrape along the ground, leading to a risk of fuel spillage and of fire. To minimize this risk, and to help protect the wing, small wheels are fitted in the bottom of each tank. Normally these wheels are covered by a fairing; in an emergency the fairing crumbles away, exposing the wheel.

The fail-safe philosophy is also incorporated in many detail parts. For example, bolts mounted vertically are assembled with the head uppermost so that if the nut should come off, or fail to be screwed on after maintenance work, they do not drop out immediately and are more likely to remain in position until the missing nut is detected. Vital bolts incorporate built-in retaining devices, in addition to the normal securing nut.

In designing detail parts, designers try to bear Murphy's Law in mind. As explained in the chapter bearing this title, this law states that "if a mechanism can be assembled incorrectly, someone, someday, will assemble it that way". Designers do their best to eliminate such possibilities.

Similar to "Murphy's Law" is the possibility that pilots may misread their instruments. The worst example of this, perhaps, concerns the altimeter, the misreading of which is believed to have caused several accidents. For many years standard altimeters had three pointers, a large one indicating hundreds, and two small ones indicating thousands and tens of thousands of feet. The design of the pointers was such that the 10,000-foot pointer could be masked by the 100-foot pointer, making it easy to misread the height by 10,000 feet. This point is ably demonstrated in the pictures on page 80. Misreading is now prevented by the use of direct reading altimeters on which numerals indicate the height. In addition a distinctive warning flag can be incorporated which appears whenever the aircraft's height is below 15,000 feet. Similar steps are being taken to improve the design and presentation of instruments displaying engine speed, some of whose early designs were easily misinterpreted.

In spite of careful design and extensive testing, when a new airliner goes into service there is a settling-down period during which unforeseen "bugs" are corrected or eliminated. These "bugs" are usually minor, but they can be serious, as in the cases of the fires on the Douglas DC-6 and the wing vibration problem on the Lockheed Electra.

The experience gained during the settling-down period is used to make the aircraft more reliable or more economical – and safer. This experience is carried over, as far as possible, in the design of new aircraft. The successful carry-over of such knowledge depends mainly on having a conscientious design staff, with a continuing background of civil aircraft experience. This emphasizes the importance of keeping design teams together.

Designers are usually successful in designing out the snags and errors of previous aircraft, but new aircraft almost always introduce new, relatively untried features which tend to generate a crop of different snags when the aircraft goes into service. The ultimate safety of air travel depends very largely on the safety measures introduced during the design stage. There is a body of opinion which considers that, in spite of the efforts currently devoted in this direction, more safety in design is required, even at the expense of profitability. This action will have to be initiated by the airlines and airworthiness authorities, and made a common requirement for all constructors, as no manufacturer can afford to "go it alone" and get out of step with his rivals.

5

On the record

The British European Airways Vanguard G-APEE arrived over London Airport just after midnight. It was very foggy. The pilot, guided by an air traffic controller on the ground, carefully lined up the big airliner for a landing on the 9,000-foot-long runway. But the fog was too dense, and the pilot, Captain N. H. Shackell, initiated an "overshoot"; that is, he opened up the throttles and went round for a second attempt. Once again the visibility was too poor, and another "overshoot" was initiated. This time the airliner was directed to join the "stack" over near-by Watford where, with its thirty passengers and crew of six, it circled patiently for about half an hour.

At about a quarter past one in the morning Captain Shackell started on his third attempt to land. It was still foggy, but the horizontal visibility, between 400 and 500 yards, was above the "minima" required for a Vanguard landing at this airport.

At twenty-three minutes past one there was a dreadful grinding noise, followed by the fierce crackle of flames. Then silence. Because of the thick fog, nobody saw what actually happened, but it quickly

became known that "Double Echo" had crashed, killing all thirty-six occupants. This accident occurred on October 27, 1965, and was the worst disaster ever for the airline, and the first fatal accident involving a Vanguard, which had entered service early in 1961.

The tragedy naturally was headlined in the newspapers the following day. Because of the circumstances, most of the air correspondents offered the theory that the pilot had either encountered a patch of very dense fog, or that he had momentarily lost sight of the runway lights as he neared the ground and his view became more oblique.

But the experienced people responsible for investigating air accidents jumped to no conclusions. They knew that the accident *could* have been caused by any one of a hundred mechanical failures, perhaps even by the pilot dying at the controls as he came in to land. They had first to be satisfied that no fault had developed in the aircraft, its instruments or its engines, on its last flight from Edinburgh, and that the pilot was alive at the moment of impact. The burned-out wreckage of the airliner was strewn along the runway for over 2,000 feet, and obtaining clues from this was not going to be an easy task. Moreover, any clues gained would not necessarily indicate just what had happened during the last few moments in the darkness and fog. In previous accidents which had resulted in severe damage and fire, investigators had all too often had to conclude that there was "not sufficient evidence upon which to make a determination of probable cause".

Amongst the wreckage of this crash, however, was a "silent witness" which was to tell the experts many of the things they wanted to know most urgently. For the aircraft had been fitted with a flight recorder, a device which recorded facts about the aircraft's behaviour and performance during its last flight, or previous series of flights. Although badly battered, the all-important wire on the spool of the flight recorder was intact and played its secrets back satisfactorily. By examining the replay, accident investigators were able to study the airspeed, altitude, magnetic heading, vertical speed and pitch attitude of the Vanguard during its last forty hours of flying.

Included were details of the last fateful flight from Edinburgh, particularly those of the last few seconds before the moment of impact. The recorder data showed, much to everyone's surprise, that the Vanguard did *not* crash while attempting to land. The pilot had initiated the overshoot manoeuvre successfully and then climbed steeply to 400 feet. The aircraft did not then stall – a theory which almost certainly would have been advanced were it not for the evidence provided by the recorder. There was no failure of the flying controls, electrical supplies or instruments, and at the moment of impact the engines were under full power. What had happened was that following the climb to 400 feet a strong "pushover" was initiated; that is, the control column was pushed forward hard to lower the nose of the aircraft, presumably to stop the aircraft from stalling. The pushover, however, was unusually prolonged, and no attempt was made to reverse it until barely two seconds before impact.

The device on the Vanguard did not record engine power or flap positions, but the accuracy of the data that was retrieved made it possible to calculate these. With this additional knowledge, the investigators were able to deduce the pilot's use of the elevator and the force he exerted on the control column; they could then reconstruct and study the sequence of events during the last eighteen seconds of the flight regarding engine power, flap position, elevator movement, control column forces and even the time lag experienced on the air-driven instruments.

The lag of response on the air-driven instruments was of vital significance because at three seconds before impact the vertical airspeed indicator was indicating a climb of 600 feet per minute, although the aircraft had actually been descending for two and one-half seconds, and the control column had been forward of neutral for four seconds. Reference by any of the pilots to another instrument, the artificial horizon, would have indicated the true picture. They did not do so, presumably because they were distracted by the incorrect movement of the flaps, which had been inadvertently selected beyond the correct 20° position to nearly straight up.

Without a recorder this valuable information would not have been available to the technicians investigating the accident, which was officially summarized as being due to the combination of a series of misfortunes, no single one of which would have caused the crash.

Another accident which dramatically illustrated the value of flight recorders was the crash of the prototype BAC One-Eleven airliner on October 22, 1963. The aircraft had taken off from the manufacturer's airfield at Wisley at 10.17 a.m. for a programme of stalling tests. After take-off it climbed to 17,000 feet and headed west, monitored by Wisley radar. At 10.26 a.m. the co-pilot reported that they were just about to commence the tests. At 10.35 a.m. he reported that four stalls had been completed in the "clean configuration", that is, with the flaps up and the landing gear retracted. At 10.36 a.m. he acknowledged a fix from Wisley, after which nothing was heard from the aircraft. Soon the sad news was received that the prototype had crashed, killing the test crew of seven, including the deputy chief test pilot, M. J. Lithgow.

As the aircraft was engaged upon the manufacturer's certification test programme, two recorders had been fitted for accident investigation purposes. One was a Midas magnetic tape recorder, capable of dealing with up to 270 inputs and on this occasion being used to record 59 items of information. It was installed in the top right side of the rear fuselage, and was designed to eject automatically when subjected to heat or immersion in water. The second recorder, from Colnbrook Instruments Development (CID), was fitted in the cabin inside a steel fireproof box. It recorded photographically on paper and gave a continuous recording of ten inputs, including altitude, indicated airspeed, acceleration, and elevator, aileron and rudder angles.

Eye-witness accounts and an examination of the wreckage showed that the rate of descent had been very high and the forward speed low. What had caused the rapid rate of descent, and what action the pilot had taken to check it, might never have become known had it not been for the vital information on the two flight recorders. The CID recorder, which had been exposed to great heat, had lost much of its information, but the trace indicating the position of the elevator remained legible.

From data provided by the recorders it was apparent that Test No. 5, a stall with the flap extended 8° and the landing gear retracted, was commenced at about 10.38 a.m. at an altitude of between 15,000 and 16,000 feet. The approach to the stall was quite normal, but during the test the angle of attack increased substantially above the figure anticipated. The flight recorders showed that the g break (the point at which the g force changes from positive to negative) at the stall was large and abrupt, causing downward acceleration and further rapid increase in angle of attack. A situation rapidly developed which was impossible for a pilot, even of Lithgow's calibre, to appreciate soon enough and therefore prevent further build-up of angle of attack.

As the angle of attack increased due to downward acceleration, the elevators (operated by small servo-tabs hinged at their trailing edges) started to trail up and this movement increased so that the effectiveness of the tailplane and elevator was reduced to a fraction of the normal value. Eventually the elevators reached the fully up position, in spite of a large push force exerted by the pilot on the control column.

The aircraft continued to descend at a high rate in a substantially horizontal attitude. During the descent it was banked twice to the right and once to the left, and at one stage the engines were opened up to full power. This latter action resulted in a large nose-up movement which, when power was taken off, apparently to prevent the pitch up increasing still further, was followed by a pitch down. The aircraft then again assumed the substantially horizontal attitude in which it hit the ground.

Subsequent wind tunnel tests and calculations showed that the aircraft had got into what is known as a "stable stall" condition, from which recovery was not possible. Even if the elevator had been fully down, it would not have provided a sufficiently large load to push the nose down so that the aircraft could recover from the stall. This characteristic is present to some degree in all aircraft with T-tails, and is accentuated in aircraft with rear-mounted engines on which the wing, being nearer the elevators, tends to blanket the tailplane.

The purpose of certification tests, which subject aircraft to stresses and strains that would not normally be encountered in ordinary use, is to ensure that the aircraft when offered to airline operators is as safe as human endeavour can make it. In the case of the One-Eleven, the elevator control mechanism was immediately altered to give a more direct mechanical connection between the pilot's control and the elevator. In addition, changes were made to the shape of the wing leading edge to improve the nose-down pitching characteristics of the aeroplane.

The need for a flight recorder to assist accident investigations was highlighted during several accidents in which either the crash was so severe that investigators were hampered by the lack of clues, or the aircraft had disappeared without trace over the open sea, leaving no clues whatsoever. The latter are particularly worrying because the manufacturers and operators of the aircraft concerned do not know whether the accident was an isolated incident due to natural causes, such as a severe thunderstorm, or was due to some malfunction which might be repeated on other aircraft.

The idea of making a running record of key flight data seems to have been initiated by the CAB in the U.S., which introduced a regulation in 1941 requiring the installation of a device to record altitude and whether the radio transmitter was on or off. The requirement was rescinded in 1944 because of the maintenance difficulties and lack of spare parts for the recorders due to the war effort. In 1947 a second attempt was made to introduce legislation, applicable to aircraft of 10,000 pounds or more, requiring the recording of altitude and vertical accelerations. This too was rescinded, as there were no suitable recorders available.

Engineers of United Air Lines became interested in the problem in the early fifties; they too discovered that there was nothing available although, rather surprisingly, a disposal concern, Waste King, was working on a gadget that showed promise. United's engineers co-operated with Waste King in developing their recorder. In addition to improving its reliability, they made it fit into the standard aircraft equipment racks, and improved its performance sufficiently for it to be used in United's fleet of jet airliners. Concurrently the CAB and the FAA continued to develop suitable requirements, and in August 1957 they issued a regulation making it mandatory after July 1958 for all aircraft weighing over 12,500 pounds and operating in airline service over 25,000 feet to carry recorders for airspeed, altitude, direction, vertical acceleration and time.

It became mandatory to fit all new British jet airliners with crash recorders from July 1965, and all older aircraft by July 1966. The British Board of Trade requires the recorders to store readings of at least six quantities, taken at intervals of one second or less. The quantities required are the aircraft's speed, altitude, and vertical acceleration, the direction it is heading in, its angle of pitch towards or away from the ground, and the time. Experts can learn a lot by correlating even these few factors; for example, a low airspeed and a steepening pitch angle, followed by a sudden downward acceleration, indicates a stall.

The equipment required to record this information which becomes priceless after an accident is comparatively simple. In the flight compartment is a control unit, used by the pilot for recording flight identification number, and for starting the recorder manually if this operation is not effected automatically. A processing unit, as its name implies, receives the various bits of information being recorded and converts them into simple electrical impulses. After processing, the data is transmitted to the recording unit, where it is stored on stainless steel wire, magnetic tape or some other medium. This unit is similar to a home tape recorder, and the recording can be played back through special equipment which converts the electrical impulses into wavy lines on a long strip of paper. The recording unit is the only part of the system that needs to be recovered after an accident; it is generally mounted in the tail of the aircraft, as this part is usually damaged least in a crash.

In order to be useful after an accident, the recorder unit itself must be sufficiently robust to survive the

crash and any fire that may follow. Recorders on
British aircraft are required to be able to withstand
an impact shock of 100 g and a temperature of 430° C
for fifteen minutes. In addition, the recording medium
must be proofed against or able to survive contact
with fluids such as fire extinguishant, Skydrol hydraulic fluid, fuel and sea water. In 1966 the FAA recorder
regulations were made even more stringent, requiring
recorders to be able to withstand 1000 g impacts, a
500 pound steel bar dropped from ten feet, a 5,000
pound crushing force applied to each side for five
minutes in sequence, and a temperature of 1,100° C.
To aid recovery, the recorders must be coloured bright
orange or yellow.

By the end of 1965, the CAB had investigated over
181 accidents involving aircraft with flight recorders
installed, and vital information from the recorded data
was obtained in 125 of these cases. Typical of the
accidents to civil airliners in which recorders have
proved useful were those of the Northwest Airlines
Boeing 720B near Miami in 1963 and the Bonanza
Air Lines Fairchild F-27A at Las Vegas in 1964.

The Northwest Boeing 720B had taken off from
Miami International Airport on February 12 at 1.35
p.m. Fifteen minutes later it disintegrated in the air
and crashed thirty-seven miles from the airport,
killing all thirty-five passengers and the crew of eight.

This crash resulted in one of the most protracted
investigations ever conducted into a civil air accident,
the proceedings lasting over two years. About 97 per
cent of the aircraft was recovered and painstakingly
reassembled in three-dimensional jig-saw fashion. The
CAB investigators, aided by engineers from Boeing,

initially considered a variety of possible causes, including an explosion, fatigue failure of a main component, a control system failure, excessive gust loading
and "flutter". The remains of engine No. 3 were examined particularly thoroughly, because it had failed
in a distinctive manner and because the engine
mounting had been repaired after an accident to the
aircraft a year earlier. All these possibilities were
eliminated as the prime cause of the accident.

The aircraft was equipped with a flight recorder,
monitoring altitude, airspeed, heading and vertical
accelerations. A study of the traces indicated that the
aircraft had encountered light turbulence soon after
take-off, followed by periods of moderate to severe
turbulence. On several occasions, when it appeared
that the turbulence was heavier, the heading trace
showed that the pilot had stopped the gentle turn
then in process to level the wings – a good technique
when penetrating rough air.

The recorder indicated that the aircraft passed out
of the heavy turbulence area at about 1.46 p.m. while
climbing through 15,000 feet. From this point to the
final manoeuvre at about 1.47 p.m., the recorder
traces showed a mild oscillating motion of the aircraft
as it climbed from 15,000 to 17,250 feet. The traces
showed that the fatal accident manoeuvre itself lasted
no more than forty-five seconds. In this brief time
interval, the big airliner climbed steeply, reaching a
climb rate about three and one-half times its normal
rate, and then pitched nose down and dived towards
the ground at high speed, when the airframe disintegrated.

Without a flight recorder, it would have been

impossible to determine and study the motions of the aircraft during this critical period. As it was, using the data recorded together with that obtained from extensive tests and analyses made during the investigation, the CAB determined with confidence that the probable cause of the accident was the unfavourable reaction of severe vertical air drafts and large longitudinal control displacements resulting in a longitudinal upset from which a successful recovery was not made.

The flight recorder evidence in the Bonanza Air Lines F-27A crash was helpful in an unusual manner, for it provided evidence of the crew's attitude regarding navigation rules in a way that no other medium could. The F-27, flying from Phoenix, Arizona, to Las Vegas, Nevada, struck high terrain while attempting an instrument approach in a snowstorm to McCarron Field, Las Vegas. All twenty-six passengers and the crew of three perished in the crash.

The accident investigation indicated that the aircraft's power-plants, flying controls and airframe systems had all been operating normally prior to impact. No icing problem appeared to have been encountered and all the navigational instruments in the aircraft and on the ground were functioning normally.

On an instrument approach to Las Vegas a widely-used system known as DME (Distance Measuring Equipment) is used to tell the pilot his distance from the station. At Las Vegas, the DME provides "fixes" at two, three, six, ten and fifteen miles from the airport; these points are shown on an approach chart carried on the aircraft, which also shows the minimum

A typical old style of three-pointer altimeter, indicating 10,000 ft.

The same three-pointer altimeter, indicating 1,000 ft.

A contemporary altimeter indicating 1,000 ft.

The flight recorder recovered from the wreckage of Vanguard 'double echo' which crashed at London Airport in October 1965. (*British European Airways*)

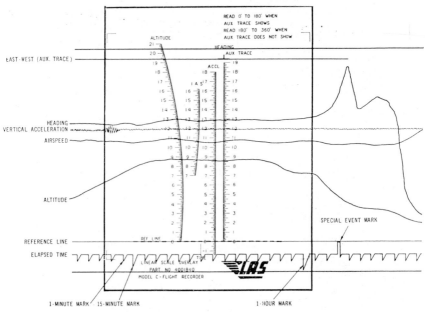

Typical trace obtained from a flight recorder fitted to a Boeing 707, shown with scale overlay.

An ejectable flight recorder developed primarily for military aircraft.

since the fuselage and the cabin break into seperate pieces. instrumentation can be damaged, but if the flight data recorder is put in to the rear of the plane it is more likely that it will be recovered. making sure these are recovered means that investigations on improving aircraft design can be successful.

Position of flight recorder in tail of aircraft.

Air traffic controllers at work (*Federal Aviation Agency*)

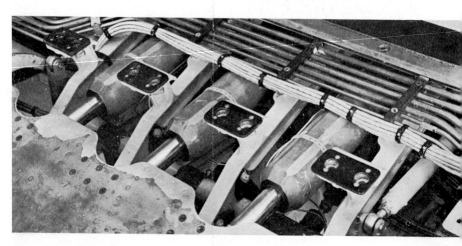

Triplexed safety: three hydraulic jacks are used to power each primary flying control surface on the Hawker Siddeley Trident.

descent altitudes to be followed between the various "fixes", there being a 6,000-foot minimum altitude between the fifteen-mile and ten-mile fixes and a 4,300-foot minimum altitude between the ten-mile and six-mile fixes. The F-27 crashed just over nine miles from the airport, striking the southern slope of a 3,525-foot hill which was well below the specified minimum altitude at that position.

The problem confronting the accident investigators was to find the cause of the fatal descent below the specified altitude. For the purpose of the investigation, the CAB initially assumed that the descent was unintentional: that is, that the pilot did not realize he had descended below the recommended altitude. This assumption made it necessary to believe that the crew's attention was diverted from altitude considerations for a period of two minutes or more after initiating the descent, and that neither pilot paid any attention to the altimeters.

However, it was considered most unlikely that the pilots, both with records of good discipline regarding compliance with rules, would have ignored altimeter indications for a period of two minutes when their intention would have been to level off approximately thirty seconds after starting the descent. Nor was there any evidence of distraction; a radio contact with Approach Control at 8.24 p.m. appeared completely routine. The investigators, therefore, rejected the assumption that the descent to 3,600 feet was unintentional, and argued that it had been a deliberate act.

A major factor contributing to this conclusion was the evidence provided by the flight recorder. The traces showed a continuous and normal descent up to the point of impact. The early part of the trace showed particularly precise compliance with altitude requirements, giving weight to the CAB's new assumption that the pilots thought that they were behaving correctly.

The question that now had to be answered was, why were the crew apparently unaware of the minimum height over this part of the approach? As previously mentioned, the minimum descent altitudes for instrument approaches are provided on charts carried on the flight decks. These charts include a plan of the approach, with the position of the various DME fixes indicated, and a section or profile of the flight path indicating the required heights between the fixes.

Initially the crew of the Bonanza F-27 had expected to make what is known as a "No. 2" type of approach, but at about 8.12 p.m. they were advised to expect a "No. 3" approach. This required a separate chart which, although similar in appearance, displayed the critical descent information in a quite different manner from all the other charts used for all other approaches, including those used for conventional VOR approaches to Las Vegas.

The approach chart carried on board the Bonanza F-27 displayed no descent information on the profile section from the fifteen-mile fix to the six-mile fix. It did, however, show a solid horizontal line between the six-mile fix and the three-mile fix, with an altitude of 3,100 feet.

The CAB investigators noted that from the time the crew of the F-27 were advised to expect a No. 3 approach to the time of starting the actual approach was nine minutes. Only nine minutes to absorb a chart presenting vital data in a subtly different manner from the style of all other charts used by the airline. That was not all, for during those nine minutes the pilots were given no less than seven instructions relating to changes in heading or altitude and were in contact with the tower on nine additional occasions for other information relating to the approach and landing conditions. During this period of sixteen interruptions the crew were also busy carrying out the pre-landing check.

The flight recorder showed that during this time the aircraft was encountering light turbulence. As the F-27 was not equipped with an auto-pilot, one of the pilots would have been concentrating practically all his attention on flying the aircraft.

It was concluded that there had been little uninterrupted time for the captain to familiarize himself with the approach procedure details, and the probable cause of the accident was officially given as the misinterpretation of the approach chart. The CAB very quickly contacted the FAA, recommending that the altitude restrictions given on the plan views of approach charts be included on the profile views so that the critical heights were more clearly identified.

Generally speaking, flight recorders to date have tended to indicate what did *not* cause an accident rather than what did. However, their assistance in tracing the causes of these two and many other accidents has indicated their enormous potential as an aid to greater safety in the air.

However, flight recording systems, although comparatively simple, are not cheap; their cost and maintenance can involve an operator in an annual expense of up to £10,000 per aircraft. Operators are therefore experimenting to see whether recorders, while recording the mandatory data required for accident investigation purposes, can simultaneously record maintenance information which would be useful on a day-to-day basis. In Britain, BEA have experimentally fitted a Vanguard with a recorder which, in addition to recording the basic "accident" data, records nine factors showing how the engines are behaving, such as revs per minute, oil pressure and temperature. The intention is to detect any deterioration in an engine's performance at the earliest possible moment, so that it can be corrected right away on the premise that "one fault cured in time may save nine". The failure of an engine rarely causes an accident, but it can be an expensive matter if, for example, it happens away from base and a spare engine has to be flown out.

In North America, Air Canada is equipping its jet fleets with the Midas system for maintenance recording, and in the U.S., TWA is installing its American equivalent, known as LMRS to avoid confusion with the Midas satellite. They and other airlines have fully adopted the philosophy of "preventive recording" which is designed to avoid accidents rather than to solve them after they have occurred.

This philosophy will be applied to an even greater extent in the supersonic airliners of the future. On these aircraft it has been suggested that the flight recorder data should be telemetered to ground-based computers, along the lines of missile and satellite technology. The computers would continuously and rapidly analyse the data, and alert the crew to any deteriorating conditions in flight, such as fuel reserves, engine, navigation and equipment malfunctions. An additional advantage of telemetered data would be rapid servicing at arrival terminals, since maintenance personnel would have advance information about any necessary replacement parts.

In addition to requiring the recording of performance data, the FAA made the recording of flight deck speech mandatory in the middle of 1966. The voice recording system is operated continuously from the start of the pre-flight check to the completion of the post-flight drill. The tape, or other recording medium, is automatically erased and re-used, and only the last thirty minutes of conversation must be available in the event of an accident.

There seems little doubt that putting things "on the record" represents a major step forward in the development of air safety. It offers one of the best means of improving air safety for a given sum of money.

6

Fitted for your safety

Passengers, quite rightly, take the basic safety features of an airliner for granted. They assume that the essential standards of strength and airworthiness have been met: that is, that the wings are strong enough to support the aircraft in flight, that the landing gear is strong enough to withstand the shocks of landing, and that the ailerons, rudder and elevator give the pilot the required degree of manoeuvrability.

A great deal of ancillary equipment, however, is also installed for the personal safety of passengers. Much of it is normally hidden from view but, like the lifeboats on an ocean-going liner, it is ready for use in an emergency.

For example, jet airliners fly high so that they are above the stormy weather often experienced at lower altitudes, and so that their engines can operate most efficiently. The airliners normally cruise between 30,000 and 40,000 feet, and at these heights the air pressure and oxygen content is too low for normal breathing. The aircraft are therefore pressurized so that, although they may be flying at 35,000 feet, the conditions in the passenger and crew compartments are equal to those at 8,000 feet. The consequences of the cabin pressure falling suddenly while an airliner is cruising at a high altitude are extremely serious; inability to breathe would soon be followed by unconsciousness and death. To ensure the passengers' safety in such an emergency, an oxygen system is fitted. Oxygen is stored, usually as a gas in high pressure cylinders from which pipelines lead to oxygen masks in the crew compartment, galleys, toilets and passenger cabins. These masks are stowed in the "passenger service units", the square panels containing the cold air outlet, reading light and steward call button, generally mounted under the coat racks above the passengers, though in some aircraft they are in the backs of the seats. Normally these masks are hidden out of sight, but should the pressure in the cabin fall below a certain level, still well within normal breathing limits, the masks automatically drop down in front of the passengers. The oxygen supply is turned on by the action of the passenger holding the mask to his face.

It is important that the flight crew have oxygen rapidly, and the masks in the crew compartment are usually of a special "quick-donning" type. De-pressurization tests have shown that they can be ejected and put on, and the wearer can be breathing oxygen within two seconds. In some circumstances, however, even this might not be quick enough; to ensure that control is maintained continually, many airlines have a rule requiring at least one flight crew member to be "on oxygen" all the time. Should a de-pressurization emergency occur, the pilot will usually descend as rapidly as he can to an altitude where normal breathing is possible.

In case a passenger is taken ill on a flight, such as an elderly person suffering a heart attack, a small portable therapeutic oxygen medical kit is carried.

Oxygen masks are never used during the entire lifetime of most airliners, but they are there, fitted for your safety.

Three-quarters of the world's surface is covered with water, and when flying long distances over water, airliners must carry life-rafts. Where only short over-water distances are involved life-rafts are not mandatory, although life-jackets must be carried if the flight takes the aircraft beyond gliding range from land. These life-jackets and rafts are of the inflatable type and during tests have proved extremely seaworthy and durable. Complementing the life-rafts are emergency rations, first-aid kits, flares and emergency radio packs or "survival beacons". The beacons are simple but sturdy transmitters which broadcast a special distress signal to enable searching aircraft and ships to locate the accident. The survival beacons are usually carried on the life-rafts and switch on automatically when immersed in the water or when the aerial is extended. The signal transmitted is modulated by an aural tone to identify it as a distress signal. A directional attachment to a normal communications set allows rescue ships and aircraft to home on to the signal.

One of the tests to which new airliners are subjected is that of "ditching". Models are used to ensure that the aircraft has satisfactory ditching characteristics: that is, that it will touch down as gently as possible and will not decelerate too violently, nor tend to break up.

Like the oxygen masks, the only "action" that most

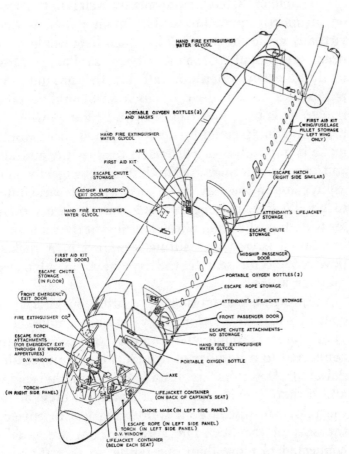

Emergency equipment fitted on board BEA Tridents.

life-jackets and rafts see is during periodic tests to
ensure they are serviceable. A forced landing in water
is an extremely rare event, but the rafts are there, just
in case, for your safety.

One item of "safety" equipment which is not carried
on airliners is parachutes. The main reason is that
virtually no accidents occur in which lives would have
been saved had parachutes been available. Most
fatalities occur when aircraft hit the ground and
parachutes would then be useless. Should a pilot
realize he is in serious trouble at a height at which a
parachute jump could be made, the high speed would
make it impossible for passengers to clear the aircraft,
and in a jet at cruising altitude the passengers would
asphyxiate on the way down anyway. For parachutes
to be effective, passengers would have to wear them
for the whole duration of the journey, at the same time
breathing oxygen and sitting strapped in a rocket-
powered ejector seat of the type used in advanced
military aircraft!

Various fire extinguishers are fitted on aircraft to
control small fires before they become serious. The
"hot" areas around the engines are permanently
connected to a number of cylinders containing extinguishant. Detectors are installed around the engine
and if there is evidence of overheating in these areas,
the pilot can discharge a suffocating gas to envelop
the seat of the fire. The spray nozzles are usually
connected to more than one bottle, so that the pilot
can have a second "shot" if the first one is ineffective.
Some extinguishers can be connected to pipes leading
to various parts of the aircraft under the floor, for
example, to the electrical and hydraulic equipment

bays and to the freight holds. Upon a warning of fire
in one of these areas, a member of the crew will
connect the fire extinguisher to the pipe leading to the
particular area and discharge the contents. For small
fires that may break out in the cabin, perhaps through
a passenger being careless with a cigarette, various
small portable fire extinguishers are fitted.

In contrast to rarely used items of equipment such
as fire extinguishers, life-rafts and oxygen masks, there
is one item of equipment fitted for the safety of
passengers that is used at least twice on every flight –
seat belts! These immensely strong belts are worn
during take-off and landing, when they greatly reduce
the chances of injury in a mishap. They are sometimes
worn while flying through turbulent weather, to
prevent passengers bumping their heads on the
ceiling.

In the event of a mishap on land, such as an aircraft
going off the end of the runway, passengers are faced
with the problem of getting out of the aircraft. To
permit emergency descents, escape ropes and escape
chutes are fitted near all the exit doors. The escape
chutes enable passengers to reach the ground by
sliding down a canvas chute. On some airliners the
escape chutes are of the inflatable type, and are
inflated from lightweight air-bottles. One end of each
chute is permanently attached to the structure near the
exit, to minimize the time necessary to get the chutes
into position.

In a crash landing the normal sources of electrical
power would cease to operate; airliners incorporate
independent lighting systems, fed from a battery, which
come on automatically in an emergency. Batteries

are also used to supply power to other essential services. The emergency system is capable of lighting the cabin interior, essential notices and emergency exits.

Because of the ever-present risk of fire, it is important that any survivors are evacuated as rapidly as possible, and airworthiness authorities have established minimum standards regarding the number and size of emergency exits to be provided. The number specified assumes that half the exits may be unusable, as would be the case if the fuselage turned on its side during the crash. To provide access to the exits, the backs of seats are designed so that an extra strong push will fold them flat, making more room.

In rare circumstances all the doors and emergency exits may be unusable, and to help rescuers to get into the cabin as quickly as possible, certain areas of the fuselage are marked "cut here". These are areas behind which there are no obstructions, and portable power saws can cut through them relatively easily. A number of small axes are fitted inside the aircraft to help free any trapped passengers, and well-equipped first-aid kits are available for treating cuts, broken limbs and burns, and even snake and spider bites.

Clearly, considerable thought is given to the provision of equipment to help ensure your safety in the event of an accident. But, as with other aspects of airliner design and operation, the amount of safety equipment carried is, and must be, the result of compromises. Some authorities and individuals, such as the impassioned crusader, B. W. Townshend, consider that the compromises currently made are weighted too much in favour of greater economy at the price of reduced safety. For example, it has been pointed out that life-rafts and life-jackets are mandatory only if the airliner is flying certain distances from the shore. Life-jackets only need be carried for distances up to 400 miles from land, depending upon the aircraft's performance. In a safe ditching, the life-jackets would almost certainly prevent passengers from drowning, but an elderly person would probably die of exposure within half an hour, because of the low temperature of the sea. Even fit young people rarely survive more than two hours' immersion. This, of course, assumes that passengers manage to don their life-jackets before their bodies go rigid, which takes about five minutes in winter time! Life-rafts are really needed to ensure a reasonable chance of survival.

Some airworthiness authorities require neither life-rafts nor life-jackets so long as aircraft remain within "gliding distance of land". But a coastline of towering cliffs may make a pilot in trouble decide to ditch in the sea rather than crash-land, as would rocky terrain or a densely populated area. The phrase in some national regulations has been changed to "land suitable for making an emergency landing", or "a suitable aerodrome where a safe landing can be made", and hopefully the rest will soon adopt this more enlightened viewpoint.

7

Collision course

"Salt Lake. United 718." "Up! Up!" "We're going in. . . ." At 10.31 a.m. on June 30, 1956, these frenzied messages were picked up by air traffic controllers at Salt Lake City and San Francisco. The abrupt end to the messages indicated one of aviation's worst disasters, the collision in mid-air over the Grand Canyon in Arizona of a Trans World Airlines Lockheed Super-Constellation and a United Airlines Douglas DC-7.

All seventy people aboard the Constellation and the fifty-eight aboard the DC-7 died. Within minutes of being notified, CAB officials were on their way to the scene of the disaster. Other officials started looking into details of the flight plans of the two aircraft.

The two airliners had left Los Angeles International Airport less than three minutes apart. The TWA Flight No. 2 was headed for Kansas City, and the United Airlines Flight No. 718 for Chicago. A thick overcast sky shrouded the California coast at the time of take-off, and both Captains had filed flight plans calling for Instrument Flight Rules (IFR). This meant that their courses would be monitored by flight controllers on the ground, that they would pass periodic check points and would receive information about other aircraft in the vicinity. The plans called for the Constellation to cruise at 19,000 feet and for the D C-7 to cruise at 21,000 feet. Similar flights had been made many times before and the trips were considered quite routine and safe. The pilot of the Constellation, in fact, had flown the route 177 times. The Constellation was to report over Daggett, California, and the D C-7 over Palm Springs to the south, when the two tracks would be some eighty miles apart. From these check points the routes converged until they crossed at the Grand Canyon, the D C-7 slightly in front of the Constellation, but a safe 2,000 feet above it.

After clearing the coastal overcast, Captain Jack S. Gandy, piloting the Constellation, asked Los Angeles Flight Control for permission to climb to 21,000 feet, presumably to avoid some rough air. At the same time he changed to VFR, that is, Visual Flight Rules. Having done so, it became his responsibility to see other aircraft which might be in the general area, rather than relying on reports from the ground. Ground control refused permission for Gandy to increase his height, because the United aircraft was assigned to the 21,000-foot level. The pilot was, however, free under flight rulings to change to VFR.

Some time later Gandy contacted Ground Control again, this time requesting permission to fly "1,000 feet on top" of the highest clouds he would encounter. It was a fine sunny morning, with a few isolated patches of cloud, and odd cumulus clouds here and there some 20,000 feet above the mile-deep Canyon floor. The Ground Controller, aware of the scattered cloud conditions along the Constellation's course, and knowing that the pilot was then flying on VFR, granted permission. The Controller warned Gandy of the oncoming United DC-7, and the warning was duly acknowledged. Owing to the pressure of other work, however, the Controller did not warn the United pilot that another aircraft had been given permission to climb to his cruising altitude.

By this time the United pilot, Captain Robert F. Shirley, had also gone on "visual" (VFR), and was heading straight for Chicago at his assigned 21,000 feet. As required in his flight plan, he reported passing several check points, and gave his estimated time of arrival over the next one, the Painted Desert line of position just beyond the Grand Canyon, as 10.34.

At this stage both aircraft passed out of Los Angeles control into the area controlled from Salt Lake City. However, as both pilots were flying on VFR they were in practice on their own, in what is known technically as uncontrolled space. The time was 10.30. At 10.31 the two aircraft collided.

Exactly why at least one of the pilots did not see the other in time to avert the disaster will never be known, but an examination of the wreckage from the two airliners enabled experts to determine their relative positions at the moment of impact. Just before the collision, the two aircraft were probably flying on very nearly parallel courses; the Constellation was cruising at about 270 knots and being overtaken by the DC-7 flying a little higher at about 288 knots. In these positions the pilot of the Constellation would not have been able to see the DC-7, nor would his co-pilot unless, as was unlikely, he had been straining to look backwards through the window on his right. In clear weather both pilots on the DC-7 should have seen the Constellation long before they caught up with it, but it is assumed that the approach was made through cloud. When dangerously close, the pilot of the DC-7 might have been able to see the lower aircraft, although it would have been outside the view of the co-pilot.

By the time the DC-7 had drawn so close that even in cloud the pilot should have seen the lower aircraft, the time he had to realize what was happening and then take correcting evasive action was a matter of seconds. However much time there was, it was obviously insufficient, and aviation suffered its worst disaster ever.

The tragedy of the collision stirred the conscience of the nation. It gave added urgency to the investigation into the problem of air traffic control which had been instigated by President Eisenhower four months previously. General Edward Curtis, retired, had been appointed as a special Presidential Assistant to study and make recommendations for overcoming the current and future problems of controlling the growing air traffic crossing the United States.

The system of airways covering the continent started in the nineteen-thirties, when it comprised three lanes zig-zagging across the country, linking all the major cities. Because of their limited range, airliners had to land frequently to refuel and pick up passengers. The existing radio communications and the teletype transmission of flight details and weather reports were adequate for comparatively short flights.

D

However, with the development of longer-range air-craft, such as the Douglas DC-6 and the Lockheed Constellation, it became possible to cross the country non-stop. The old, rather informal, method of control began to grow inadequate. Pilots, taking advantage of the longer range of their newer aircraft, began to depart from the old zig-zag routes and fly more directly to their destinations. They also tended to fly much higher than before, partly to get above the weather, and partly to take advantage of the strong winds not found at lower altitudes.

The public's enthusiastic acceptance of flight produced rapid expansion in the air transportation industry. The number of airliners rose sharply, as did the number of privately-owned light aircraft, which approached 50,000. In addition, a large number of military aircraft were in the air at all times. The greater number and higher speeds of all these aircraft demanded that the timing and courses of flights should be regulated far more strictly than before. The control of the congested airways and terminal areas became America's primary air safety problem.

For these aircraft, and for the new generation of jet airliners, the Curtis commission recommended the installation of long-range radar installations and directional radio aids. With the Grand Canyon accident in mind, Congress loosened its purse-strings. This was the same Congress which in 1953 and 1954 had approved a severe cut-back in air traffic control funds. There were those who wondered uneasily if these cut-backs might have helped to perpetuate the conditions which had enabled the collision to take place. Appropriations for the air traffic control system jumped from an inadequate £5 million in 1956 to a somewhat more realistic £25 million in 1957. In 1960 the FAA was allotted nearly £40 million for new radar equipment. By the end of 1966 over £500 million had been spent on the air traffic control problem. More money and more effort has been spent in this single field than on all other civil aviation projects combined.

However, although air traffic control expanded rapidly, its facilities barely kept pace with the increase in air traffic.

In May 1958 an Air Force jet fighter collided with a United DC-7 over Las Vegas, killing all forty-nine people aboard the airliner. One month later a National Guard jet hit a Capital Airlines Viscount, killing all twelve passengers on the airliner. Both airliners were operating under Air Traffic Control on approved flight plans and were on course, at the correct altitudes in federal airways. Both military aircraft were operating under see-and-be-seen visual flight rules. The new procedures had been designed primarily to protect airliners from each other; military aircraft were still largely a law on their own.

These two collisions emphasized the need for military operations to be brought under the air traffic control umbrella, and also pointed out the inability of human vision to cope with increased flying speeds. The view from airliners was compared by one pilot to the view obtained through the narrow slit of a mail box. But even if an approaching aircraft is seen, the closing speeds are so great as to make evasion very difficult, if not impossible. One pilot described an oncoming aircraft as resembling a "fly on the wind-shield", adding "when the fly sprouts wings, you've had it".

At the beginning of 1960, there were about 2,000 civil transports operating in the United States, together with 70,000 so-called general aviation private and business aircraft and 42,000 military aircraft. At the airports which had FAA control towers (about 8 per cent of the country's airports) there were nearly *thirty million* aircraft movements. No one has even begun to estimate how many flights were generated at the remaining 92 per cent of the airports.

Another major collision occurred in December 1960. Nine days before Christmas, a United Airlines DC-8 and a Trans-World Airlines Super Constellation collided over New York City, causing the death of 127 passengers and eight people on the ground. The Constellation was approaching La Guardia Airport, its progress being monitored on a radarscope. Suddenly the controller spotted something else and flashed a warning: "Unidentified target approaching you . . . six miles . . . jet traffic." "Roger," acknowledged the TWA aircraft. A second warning that the unidentified aircraft was three miles away was also acknowledged. Then it was too late, and an outboard engine of the jet airliner smashed into the Constellation's fuselage.

The investigators concluded that the probable cause of the collision was the failure of the DC-8's crew to report that one of its two key radio navigation instruments was out of order, so that the pilot was unable to determine his exact position soon enough. In spite of the official CAB report, however, it was clear that deficiencies in air traffic control had contributed to the tragedy. A great deal of money and effort had gone into developing safe multi-lane aerial motorways, but comparatively little had been done about the one-lane traffic at the ends of the airways. Even further radical action was necessary to prevent airborne traffic jams from becoming as commonplace as those of autos on the ground.

The action came in March 1961, when President Kennedy requested the FAA to "conduct a scientific, engineering review of our aviation facilities and related research and development, and to prepare a practicable long-range plan to ensure efficient and safe control of all air traffic within the United States".

To carry out this assignment, a Task Force was appointed and six months later the FAA submitted its report, known as Project Beacon, to the President. Many of the recommendations concerned equipment and ideas already under study by the FAA. As the great majority of collisions occur near airports, attention was concentrated on reducing the hazards present at the larger terminal areas, such as New York, Los Angeles, Chicago and Washington. The hazard is caused not only by the concentrated volume of traffic, but by the constantly climbing and descending mixture of airline traffic and light aircraft. Beacon recommended the segregation of aircraft according to capability along climb and approach corridors to and from the airways. To separate light aircraft, propeller-driven airliners and jet airliners at large airports, three approach corridors and three departure corridors were proposed. "Circuits and bumps" training should not be allowed except for airfield familiarization in off-peak periods.

Beacon emphasized that to ensure complete safety between the airports, position information on all

aircraft must be continuously available, stating that
this information must be derived on the ground, or
automatically received from the aircraft, or both, and
that it must not be dependent only upon the pilot's
navigational information.

Because of the importance and volume of private
and business aircraft, due consideration was given to
this class of traffic. A major decision for Beacon concerned the degree of integration between civil airways
radar and the vast military SAGE defence system.
Although some form of co-ordination seemed logical,
the practical difficulties were greater than generally
appreciated. Not least were the maintenance ex-
penses, estimated to be £250 million annually.

Today, six years and some £300 million after
President Kennedy's initial request, the major recommendations of Beacon have been put into practice,
giving the U.S. the most advanced system of air
traffic control in the world. Traffic within thirty miles
of an airport is controlled by one of more than 300
FAA airport control towers. En-route traffic on the
airways is controlled by twenty-one Air Route Traffic
Control Centres, located strategically throughout the
country. Each centre and tower handles traffic within
its own area, using radar and radio to keep aircraft
moving safely. As the flight progresses, control is
transferred from centre to centre, and from centre to
tower.

In addition there is a third air traffic facility, the
Flight Service Station, that devotes most of its attention to more than 300,000 non-airline pilots (more
than 95 per cent of all active civil pilots) and to a
large percentage of military pilots. About 400 of these

stations and combined station towers are dotted around the nation, each covering an area of roughly 400 square miles. At the Flight Service Stations, specialists on their area's terrain provide pre-flight and in-flight briefings, weather reports, suggested routes, altitudes, and any other information important to the flight's safety. If an aircraft is overdue at its reporting station or destination, the Flight Service Station starts a search and rescue operation. If a pilot is lost or in trouble, the station gives orientation instructions and directions to the nearest emergency landing field.

To complement the improvements in air traffic control, the FAA has made it mandatory for certain airliners to carry two new navigation aids. One is known as a transponder, a radio device tied in to the ATC system. Signals transmitted from the ground are received by a transponder on the aircraft. The transponder then transmits a coded signal to ground radar which enlarges the aircraft's radar blips and makes positive identification of the blip possible.

The second aid is Distance Measuring Equipment, known as DME. This transmits a signal to a ground navigation station, which returns a signal telling the pilot exactly how far he is from the station. The distance is shown on a tiny meter, which ticks off the miles like the mileometer in a motor-car.

At the time of the Grand Canyon disaster, the Air Traffic Control System could positively control only 10,000 flights a day. Now it can accommodate nearly 23,000 flights. On the military side the FAA, with Air Force co-operation, has established fifteen "climb-corridors" for fighter-interceptors, to keep them from encroaching on commercial airways.

The first elements of a semi-automatic air traffic control system have been introduced in New York, and some other large airports. The system consists of a computer which records the speeds, arrival times, location, altitudes and direction of air traffic; previously each air traffic controller had to work out and record this information for himself, transferring the data to crude racks and paper flight strips. Future plans involve an all-electric system in which details of all controlled flights are fed into a computer, which digests and records the plans and automatically transmits them to every Air Traffic Control centre affected by any of the individual flights.

In Britain, air traffic control can be said to have started when early aviators found they needed someone to keep back the crowds and indicate when it was clear to take off. When several aircraft were operating from the same airfield it was necessary to know whose turn it was to take off or land. Royal Air Force Stations introduced a duty pilot who checked aircraft in and out. Often a pilot heading for another station would ask the duty pilot to telephone to warn them of his arrival; this grew into a departure and arrival notification system.

The development of radio introduced navigational assistance in the form of direction-finding bearings for en-route fixing and homing. This service rapidly became an essential part of air traffic control as commercial aviation developed during the twenties and thirties.

Pilots soon discovered that air traffic control could provide more help if it had advance information of a flight. It could obtain weather reports, avoid take-off delays and also alert the destination airfield and en-route navigation service. Equally important, ATC could sort out the problems which arose if more than one aircraft wanted to take off at about the same time and follow the same route. A system of Flight Plans and a procedure to be followed emerged, providing the foundation from which the present procedural control has developed. In the late thirties a crude form of airway or corridor system came into operation.

The start of the 1939–45 war initially produced some set-backs, such as radio restrictions leading to a return to signal pistols and Aldis lamps. Subsequently enormous improvements were made, a wide variety of techniques being introduced to provide en-route, homing and landing aids. Of these radar was the most important, but also valuable were the marshalling, let-down and approach systems, many of which have been further developed and are in world-wide use today. During the last months of the war, the U.S. Air Force operated an airway system for their aircraft flying between London, Brussels and Paris.

After the war came the expansion of commercial aviation, and the rebirth of the civil air traffic control. Radar control was introduced for navigational and approach guidance, but proved unable to provide at the same time the safe separation required on high density routes. It was replaced by a system based on procedural control in a series of airways, control zones and control areas, with radar playing a supporting role. The airways system came into being on August 1, 1950, when the London–Shannon airway was inaugurated. This was followed by airways linking London with Amsterdam, Brussels and Paris, and the whole system was completed with the introduction of the Scottish airways in 1951.

To prevent head-on collisions a simple rule is followed by pilots of civil aircraft. Known as the "quadrantal" rule, it requires aircraft flying on courses between north and east to cruise at heights of odd thousands of feet, for example, 7000 or 9000 feet. Aircraft on courses between south and west cruise at even thousands of feet. Thus, aircraft flying towards each other are always separated by 1000 feet of altitude. Aircraft flying on north-westerly and south-easterly courses fly at even and odd thousands of feet plus 500 feet respectively, so that there are always 1,000 feet of height separation between aircraft approaching one another and 500 feet of separation between aircraft passing at right angles.

This rule was adopted internationally in 1946 and in 1966 was changed to what is known as the "semi-circular" rule. Broadly, under this new rule, aircraft flying under visual flight rules at altitudes up to 29,000 feet on courses from 0° to 179° cruise at odd thousands plus 500 feet, and aircraft flying courses from 180° to 359° cruise at even thousands plus 500 feet; the effect is to ensure 1,000 feet of clearance between aircraft whatever their courses. At heights above 29,000 feet the clearance is 2,000 feet.

The military ATC service, with its broader requirements, established radar ATC units for its aircraft flying on routes outside the airways. Close liaison with the civil ATC centres was maintained to provide a safe airways crossing service.

In 1958, a five-year plan of air traffic control improvements was initiated. This called for radar coverage for all the airways from 5,000 feet up, providing greatly increased capacity and accuracy of control.

In the seven years from 1957 to 1964, civil air transport movements over Britain increased by nearly 50 per cent. During this period the range of speeds of civil aircraft widened, the top speed rising from around 300 knots to nearer 600 knots. Thus, not only were air traffic controllers faced with a significant increase in the number of aircraft, but in many cases the time available for the solution of control problems was roughly halved because of the increase in speeds. The even higher speeds of military aircraft reduced the time factor still further.

To overcome these problems the National Air Traffic Control Services (NATCS) was formed in 1962 to introduce a unified system of control able to look after the differing needs and speeds of civil and military aircraft. To deal with the even more complex future problems posed by the projected increase in the numbers of aircraft and in their speeds, the NATCS is installing an advanced computer to permit the automation of air traffic control. This revolutionary equipment, code-named Mediator, will simplify the task of the air traffic controllers, provide the additional capacity needed for the expansion of air traffic in the nineteen-seventies and will pave the way for the introduction of supersonic transport.

When Mediator is complete, all civil and military aircraft entering British airspace will have to file a statement of the purpose of its flight. These may vary from a very detailed flight plan of a civil airliner flying on a fixed route, to a much simpler statement from a military aircraft on a training flight. These statements about the flight will be fed into a computer along with meteorological data and details of the performance of the aircraft. A nation-wide network of radars will automatically feed information into the computer system about the position, speed and height of each aircraft while it is in British airspace. The computer will then calculate the times at which each aircraft should pass all the reporting points on its course, and will route this information to the appropriate controller's station at the relevant Air Traffic Control Centre. The computer will also continually make projections and warn controllers of potentially dangerous situations before they arise. As each reporting point is passed, the actual time will be fed into the computer, to correct the estimated times of arrival at subsequent reporting points.

At the Control Centres, each controller will be provided with a continuous up-to-date picture of the progress and intentions of the aircraft under his control. The information will be displayed in "written" form on television-like screens, which incorporate a series of "touch-wires" – the ends of tiny wires embedded in the screen. The controller can request information from the computer or modify the flight plans or make decisions simply by touching the touch-wires beneath the relevant items on the display. The computer will then change the display, either to provide the information called for, or to show the effects of a change or of a decision.

The touch-wires can also be used to request more detailed information. For example, a screen may display a list of all the aircraft flying along a particular route. The touch-wires will enable the controller to select more detailed information on any one of these aircraft. Seconds later, the touch-wires could be used to call up a display of reporting points, and the times at which this and other aircraft will pass them. Controllers will also have immediate access to detailed knowledge of all other aircraft in their area, and will be able to communicate instantly with the controllers of these aircraft should any potential loss of safe separation occur.

Apart from the extensive use of touch displays, information will be passed to the controllers in a variety of other forms. Strip printers will produce "Flight Progress Strips" for each sector controller. These slips of paper will provide the basic information for the existing method of air traffic control. Electronic tabular displays will provide an instantaneously updated display of similar information on a number of aircraft passing over a given route or reporting point. Page printers will produce a continuous summary of all information in the system. This summary will be available to the Planning Controllers and will also provide a permanent record of all aircraft movements, and the control procedures used to handle them.

With so much vital information stored in and being obtained from an electronic memory, the serious consequences of a breakdown of the computer can be imagined. To ensure reliability three computers will be used, each forming the basis of a separate processing chain, to provide a fully triplicated system in which an interruption in processing lasting more than thirty seconds is not likely to occur more than once every five years. This triplication virtually guarantees there will be no failures of any consequence.

The system is capable of future extension to link with similar control centres throughout Europe and the rest of the world. Advanced plans have already been formulated by the International Civil Aviation Organization for a fully integrated, world-wide, air traffic control system to provide the degree of international automation which will be essential in the supersonic age.

8

Riddle over the Mediterranean

The fourteen passengers reclined in their comfortable seats aboard one of the British Overseas Airways Corporation's famous Comets, the first jet airliner in the world. They were among the select few who had tasted the extraordinary smoothness and quietness of this new form of air travel which, within a few years, would make vibrating piston-engined airliners as out of date as yesterday's newspapers.

On the flight deck Senior Captain Mostert, with over 10,000 flying hours in his log book, glanced at the array of instruments in front of him as the Comet neared the end of its long climb; engine r.p.m., engine temperature, fuel contents, cabin temperature and pressure – all was well and everything working as it should be. He had taken off from Rome Airport on April 8, 1954, at 6.32 p.m. and was climbing to his recommended cruising altitude of 35,500 feet on his way to Cairo, the next stop on the long flight to Johannesburg. He switched on his radio and transmitted the following message to his destination: "I am bound for Cairo, where my estimated time of arrival is 21.20. I am ascending to 35,500 feet."

That was the last message Captain Mostert sent. In the bright sunlight high above the Mediterranean something dreadful happened, and quickly the waves swallowed up the remains of the airliner, its crew, its steward and stewardess and the fourteen passengers.

It was not fully believed that disaster had befallen the Comet until the time in which the airliner would have used up all its fuel had passed without any further news. Once it was understood, action followed swiftly. Sir Miles Thomas, Chairman of BOAC, grounded his airline's fleet of Comets nine hours after the last signal from the airliner. Aircraft of a particular type are not normally grounded when one of them has an accident; the decision is made in the light of the prevailing circumstances. On this occasion, it was prudent to ground all the aircraft as only eleven weeks previously another Comet had crashed mysteriously after taking off from Rome. Its remains too were lying hidden beneath the waters of the Mediterranean.

No time was lost in preparing for the investigation. The circumstances in which the two crashes had occurred were so similar that it seemed reasonable to assume that the cause was the same. But what was the cause?

As in all investigations the investigators considered some of the causes of previous accidents. Was it sabotage? The fact that both aircraft had taken off from the same airport in an area of political violence made this a possibility. Had some vital part of the structure or system failed? Did an empty fuel tank, full of fumes and affected by changes in pressure and temperature, explode? Or had the hydraulic system leaked, to be ignited by an electric spark? The aircraft was refuelled from underneath the wing, the fuel being pumped in to the tanks under pressure; had it been refuelled incorrectly, so that the pressure of the fuel somehow weakened the wing? Fuel may sometimes spill from an airliner's tanks during take-off and the early stages of the climb; had it ignited in the air and caused a disastrous fire?

A list of "possible causes" peculiar to jet-propelled aircraft was also studied. On take-off, as the pilot lifted the nose of the aircraft, the searing efflux from the jet engines hit the ground and was deflected up again to strike the tail of the aircraft. Had this weakened the structure so that later it failed in the air? Perhaps the rapidly spinning turbine wheel of one of the airliner's Ghost turbojet engines had broken and punctured the pressure cabin, which then would have burst like a pricked balloon. Even the remote possibility that the airliner might have been struck by a meteorite, the result of which would be the same as being struck by a high-velocity shell, was considered.

After air crashes ordinary people often contact the authorities, stating their beliefs about the causes of the accident; these amateur solutions are rarely of value, for the subject is too technical. On this occasion, because of the widespread interest in the Comet, suggestions came from all over the world. One person was quite certain that the airliner had been destroyed by a flying saucer, manned by visitors from another world who were worried about man's progress in the conquest of the air. Others claimed that the disaster was an Act of God in revenge for the world's disobedience and evil; accident investigators have come to expect such statements. Other suggestions, however, were surprisingly close to what was later found to be the actual cause.

The only initial clue was that after nearly two years of highly successful service, two Comets had crashed in quick succession under strangely similar circumstances, both while climbing about half an hour after take-off. This bare fact was by no means sufficient for an investigation, although the time lapse of two years proved to be a significant clue. Before any progress could be made it was necessary to have the wreckage for a detailed examination. Salvage operations, in fact, had already started on the first Comet which had crashed off Elba.

The British Naval forces stationed in Malta, who were assigned to the salvage operation, were confronted with two major difficulties: first, the problem of locating wreckage somewhere within an area of several hundred square miles, and second, the task of salvaging wreckage from the sea bed some 500 feet below the surface, 300 feet below the depth at which Navy divers could operate.

Locating the aircraft was not easy, for the few eye-witness reports differed by as much as ten miles. An initial estimate of the probable point of contact was calculated from the position at which some of the bodies had been recovered by fishermen, taking into account that they had been drifting for five or six hours, and that it took the little fishing boats travelling at six knots about two hours to reach port. This estimate, plus plots made from eye-witness reports, narrowed the search down to an area of approximately ten miles by ten miles! The next step was simple but monotonous; ships would sweep the whole area, like a tractor ploughing a field, until it had all been sounded. The five trawlers engaged in the search simply dragged cables along the sea bed in the hope of hooking something, but the Navy ship used her Asdic echo-sounding equipment. When the Asdic "pinged", indicating that the ship was passing over something of significant size on the bottom, a marker buoy was dropped overboard. These marked the points at which the actual salvage ships would try their luck. For the salvage operations, a giant eight-toothed grab with jaws ten feet wide was sent from England, along with an under-water television camera and a deep-sea observation chamber.

After a few days the men watching the television monitor screen thought that the camera had located the lost airliner's engines. A closer look however, revealed that the objects were Greek or Roman urns, lying in the mud as they probably had done for a thousand years or more. The first part of the aircraft was located by the camera on February 12, after five fruitless days of scouring a "ping" area.

After the location came the "salve". The procedure adopted was that developed by the Italians, who had accumulated a great deal of experience in deep-sea salvage. For success the salvage ship had to be very accurately positioned, for a grab missing a piece of wreckage by a few inches might as well miss by a mile. To hold their ships the Italians used eight mooring lines, spaced equally round the ship like the radial lines of a spider's web.

The first piece of wreckage was grabbed and raised quite easily, and this gave a false impression of the task's simplicity. For the next success did not come easily. A collection of twisted metal and iron came up, rubbish not even connected with the Comet. Two days later the area was completely bare.

And so the trawlers trawled, the Navy ship used its Asdic, men peered out of portholes in the observation chamber, and the television camera with a field of view covering only a few square feet literally inched from left to right, searching and searching. As the weeks passed the patience and care of the searchers was rewarded now and again as another piece of wreckage was first located and then retrieved, to be sent to England for detailed examination. The recovery of the four engines, which were located on the seabed near the two main wing spars, was of primary importance, as was that of the undercarriage, sections of the fuselage and the inboard stumps of the wings. One of the last vital pieces recovered was the entire front of the fuselage complete with the cockpit, flying controls, fire indicators and the cabin right back to the leading edge of the wing.

Later on in the search, in an endeavour to locate specific pieces of wreckage particularly required by the investigators, hundreds of scale models were made. These had a wing span of about three feet and were made so that the major components were held together by loose pins, to which were attached strings of varying lengths. These models were then catapulted from a balloon, eight hundred feet up, and the strings pulled the pins out in a pre-determined sequence and freed the components as they were thought to have broken off the real airliner. As the pieces fluttered to the ground, their paths were tracked with movie cameras. These experiments showed that many parts fell in a specific pattern; missing pieces were thus assumed to be in approximately the positions indicated by this pattern, and searches were made in the corresponding scaled-up areas at sea with a certain amount of success.

An effort was made to salvage the second Comet, G-ALYY, which had crashed on its way to Cairo, but it was beyond recovery, resting in water over 3,500 feet deep close to the volcanic island of Stromboli.

Simultaneously, work was proceeding in England, where the accident investigation had been placed in the hands of the Royal Aircraft Establishment, the British aviation research centre, at Farnborough. In Parliament Prime Minister Sir Winston Churchill directed that the cost must be reckoned neither in money nor in manpower, and it became the greatest investigation into an air accident the world had known.

Sir Arnold Hall, the Establishment's director, was convinced that the truth of the mystery would only be solved in the laboratory. He knew that a preconception of the cause was fatal in an air accident investigation, calling it "the almost certain way to get a wrong answer". To help with the investigations he asked for three Comets and their crews. In a specially erected canvas hangar, the laborious task of rebuilding the Comet was begun, as it was recovered piece by piece from the waters off Elba. Over a thousand men were standing by, prepared to work on the Comet mystery.

The outer fuel tanks were integral with the wing, and the possibility that incorrect refuelling techniques might have weakened the wing was checked. Water was pumped into the wing of one of the Comets allotted to Farnborough for the investigation, and the wing failed at a pressure of nine pounds per square inch. Could the refuelling trucks have delivered fuel at this pressure? One of the Italian trucks used at Rome was sent to Farnborough where, working flat out, it could pump one hundred and twenty gallons a minute, a pressure of twenty pounds per square inch. However, it was discovered that other pumps down the route could pump two hundred gallons a minute at double the pressure of the Italian truck, but that in any case the special escape vents in the tanks prevented pressures of anything like nine pounds being reached. So the refuelling procedure was deleted from the list of "possible causes".

The investigators then wanted to check on the possibility that fuel spilling from the wing during take-off might have caused a disastrous fire later in the climb. In tracing a fuel overflow the normal procedure is to paint the suspected areas with white paint, dye the fuel, conduct the test and then examine the patterns traced by the dribbling fuel afterwards. With the Comet this method could not be used as it was not possible to paint the areas inside the wing where the fuel was believed to spill. Sir Arnold Hall contacted the Atomic Research Station at Harwell, in Berkshire, to enquire whether the fuel could be specially treated to make it slightly radioactive and any spillage traced with a Geiger counter. They replied that it could be done, and soon a guinea pig Comet was taking off with radioactive fuel. When the Geiger counters were set to work it was found that fuel spilled from the tank venting system collected inside the wing, and then trickled down the trailing edge of the flaps to a point close to the jet pipe shrouds, creating a slight fire hazard. However, the investigators were convinced this had not caused the accident off Elba, as there was no evidence of fire in the vicinity of the wreckage of the wings.

What about the theory that jet blast at take-off might have damaged the rear of the fuselage? The effect of the exhaust gases could be serious enough to induce fatigue on the metal skin very quickly. It was pointed out that this effect had been allowed for shortly after the Comet went into service, and that the manufacturer had worked out a satisfactory repair scheme which had been applied on all aircraft. Thus, jet blast damage did not seem to be the cause of the accident.

To obtain data on loads imposed in the air, one of the Comets was stripped of its comfortable seats and other luxury furnishings, and fitted instead with over a hundred pieces of delicate flight test equipment. Then the aircraft was taken aloft as many as four times a day, executing manoeuvres to see if some sudden movement of the controls by the pilots of the crashed airliners could have somehow overstrained the structure. For some of the tests the aircraft was flown very fast up to the point where buffeting and flutter commenced. Flutter has caused many crashes, and although it should not have happened on the Comets, the investigators thought the stage might have been reached by mishandling, or through the airliners striking severe air turbulence. The tests gave the airliner a clean bill of health from this aspect. The investigators also considered the possibility of a member of the crew tripping in the cockpit and, in trying to steady himself, accidentally pulling the control column back sharply. It was thought that this might cause a high-speed stall in a fraction of a second. However, tests first in a flight simulator, and then in a Comet in the air, showed the Comet quite satisfactory in this respect.

The flying on the Comet loaded with test equipment involved a certain degree of risk. Two similar aircraft had crashed and pilots were deliberately submitting a third to loading conditions far beyond those experienced in service to help scientists to find out the cause. On the test flights the Comet was always followed by a Canberra, whose crew kept a close watch on the airliner for any sign of fire or loosening structure. To reduce the risk the Comet used was a relatively new one, with half the number of flying hours of the two that had crashed. The test flights were also made unpressurized which, while it may have made the flights safer, also made them much more uncomfortable. Two of the crew developed "bends", the terrible pain in bone joints caused by dissolved nitrogen in the blood turning into bubbles as a result of the decreased pressure.

In addition to the data obtained in actual flight, information of a vital nature was also gained with the third of the three Comets allotted to Farnborough. This aircraft, Yoke Uncle, was being subjected to the most stringent test of all. The fuselage of a complete aircraft had been immersed in a huge 250,000-gallon water tank, erected for the investigation. Once submerged, the airliner began to make a series of ghostly

"flights", each one lasting only five minutes, but re-
producing in that time all the major stresses incurred
on an actual three-hour journey. Massive hydraulic
pistons under the wings, which protruded through
the sides of the water tank, exerted a pressure equal
to the loads carried by the wings in flight, bending the
wings up noticeably. To simulate the pressurization,
or "blowing-up", of the cabin, water was pumped
into the cabin until the pressure had built up to eight
and a quarter pounds per square inch, the pressure
experienced by an airliner flying at 36,000 feet. This
pressure was maintained for about three minutes and
then lowered to simulate the aircraft landing. At the
same time the pistons under the wings retracted to
unload the wings. Then the cycle was repeated all
over again. While the Comets were in service BOAC
periodically tested the cabins to a pressure of eleven
pounds a square inch. To reproduce this maintenance
test, the investigators at Farnborough carefully subjected their aircraft to this special test every thousand
flights. The major advantage of this tank test was the
speed at which "flight" experience was accumulated.
In one day the submerged airliner was able to reproduce the effects of thirty-six days flying on actual
aircraft. The tank is shown on page 128.

While the aircraft was "flying" day in and day out,
the wreckage retrieved from the sea off Elba was
being carefully reassembled at Farnborough and was
beginning to provide significant clues. For example,
no evidence of a bomb-type of explosion could be
found, which effectively ruled out the possibility that
the airliner had been sabotaged. Fire, which had been
high on the list of "possible causes", was also ruled

out on the evidence of the wreckage; the proof was provided by two pieces of wreckage from the same part of the fuselage which showed clearly that they had broken up before the fire started. This finding corroborated the Italian doctor's report on the bodies salvaged from the sea. At the time the doctor had been convinced that the passengers and crew had died quickly, "by violent movement and explosive decompression", not by burning. None of the victims had drowned.

The reconstruction of the retrieved airliner was not an easy task. A wooden skeleton, ninety feet long, was made, and as the various pieces of fuselage and wing were identified they were wired into position. Some of the large bits were easy to locate, but others, small and twisted beyond recognition, were identified only after some skilful detective work. Odd blue marks on the tailplane which had survived several weeks immersion in the sea puzzled the investigators for a time. When analysed under the microscope in the laboratory it was discovered that the blue matched the material out of the seat covering; a seat forced out by the explosion had hit the tailplane and sliced right through it.

Initially, the reconstructed aircraft gave few clues to the *cause* of the disaster, but did indicate the sequence of events in those few seconds when the aircraft broke up. In the tail cone at the extreme rear of the fuselage, shreds of carpet from the cabin floor were found, together with tiny pieces of passengers' luggage and the corner of a mirror from one of the ladies' toilets. The investigators deduced that the rear end of the fuselage had broken off more or less complete and had shattered on hitting the sea, the force of the impact forcing these items up into the tail cone.

The engines of aircraft involved in accidents are always examined minutely. Investigators of the Comet noted that the turbine wheel of the port inner engine had broken away. Examination of the three remaining engines disclosed that their turbines too were on the point of failure; cracks were evident in the same regions as those in which the turbine of the port inner engine had failed. The extraordinary similarity of these defects indicated that the damage had almost certainly been caused *after* the aircraft broke up, and was not the primary cause of failure. The investigators concluded that the damage had most likely resulted from a very sudden nose-down motion while the engines were running normally. At speed the compressor-turbine assembly acted as a gyroscope and a nose-down movement would produce gyroscopic forces tending to bend the shafts sideways, and then induce failure.

To prove this theory, a Comet Ghost engine was mounted on a special framework which could be pivoted. The engine was run at normal speed, and the framework was then tilted downward to reproduce the action of an airliner nosing down in a fraction of a second. After the test the engine was found to be damaged in the same way as those recovered from the crashed airliner.

As further pieces of the Comet were salvaged and placed in position, the sequence of failure became clear, though the cause was still obscure. It seemed that the cabin had failed, causing the rear end of the fuselage to break off and then the nose, followed by the outer sections of the wings. All four portions broke off in a downward direction, leaving the main cabin and wing centre section on their own; these caught fire as they tumbled towards the sea.

But what had caused the parts to break away in the first instance? The answer came on June 24, from the airliner being tested in the water tank. Having "flown" almost nine thousand hours, the aircraft was undergoing one of its periodic tests to eleven pounds instead of eight and a quarter, when the needle on the pressure gauge suddenly dropped back to zero. The cabin was no longer holding its pressure! Nothing could be seen through the water, so the tank was hurriedly drained. When it was empty it was found that the metal skin of the cabin had split over a length of eight feet and a depth of three. Only the fact that water is virtually incompressible had prevented the aircraft from blowing to bits like a burst balloon. Initial failure was traced to a crack in the skin at the lower rear corner of an escape hatch. The fracture was immediately subjected to microscopic analysis which proved without doubt that the cause was metal fatigue.

This episode did not by itself pinpoint metal fatigue as the cause of the actual accidents, but with this vital piece of evidence, the investigators searched for back-up clues on the reassembled wreckage. Traces of fuselage paint across the line of fracture where the outer portion of the wings had broken off proved that the wing had been intact when struck by a piece of fuselage. Attention concentrated on the fuselage. Soon afterwards, in the middle of August, the salvaged cabin roof arrived at Farnborough, and in the twisted mass of metal was found a piece of skin in which a prime crack had occurred. Meticulous examination of the crack showed that it had fractured, like the skin of the aircraft tested under water, through fatigue.

What had happened to the airliner as it climbed into the peaceful sky over the Mediterranean was that the pressurized cabin had burst as though a bomb had exploded inside it. First a large section of the cabin blew out of the side, leaving the tell-tale streaks of paint across the wing. The stricken airliner then swung into a near-vertical position, when the wings snapped off under the sudden loads, followed by the tail unit and fuselage nose. The centre-section, by now burning fiercely, spiralled down into the sea.

The cause at long last had been found: metal fatigue, due to the repeated pressurizing of the fuse-lage. The cabin had been statically strong enough to withstand pressures of over nineteen pounds per square inch, but it was not capable of withstanding a pressure of slightly more than eight pounds applied repeatedly.

So ended an investigation unparalleled in the history of aviation. During the investigation three aircraft had been destroyed or damaged, hundreds of models and elaborate pieces of equipment had been made and special tests carried out. Several million pounds of money had been spent. The full report of the accident ran to 800,000 words and was contained in a folder ten inches thick.

The results of this massive investigation had far-reaching effects on the development of other aircraft, both existing and projected, in Britain and abroad. At least one well-known aircraft, which had just entered service, was subjected to a tank test of the type developed during the Comet investigation, and failed at a figure much lower than the manufacturers believed possible. Urgent strengthening modifications were carried out immediately to prevent failure due to pressure fatigue.

It is acknowledged that the enquiry provided information of particular benefit to other manufacturers of large civil aircraft such as the Boeing 707 and Douglas DC-8 series of jet airliners. The lessons learned during the investigation had a profound influence on the design of all pressure cabins developed since that time. Manufacturers of all nations were warned that even a small tear occurring when a fuselage is pressurized can result in decompression and disastrous failure. The cabins of contemporary airliners working at this level of differential pressure have thicker skinning and smaller windows; they also incorporate crack "stoppers", which are designed to prevent any crack that should occur from extending unimpeded along the cabin skin, and so to prevent catastrophic failure. In addition, the enquiry emphasized the importance of cut-outs in pressure cabins and pointed the way to more representative testing of both complete cabins and small samples.

The solution to the riddle over the Mediterranean resulted in a most significant advance in the development of structural safety in the air. No other airliner has ever again directly failed through pressure fatigue.

9

The hazard of fire

The United Airlines new DC-6 took off from Los Angeles on time, and set a course for Chicago. Cruising at 19,000 feet under visual flight rules, the pilot, Captain E. L. McMillan, gave routine progress reports over Fontana, Dogget, Silver Lake, Las Vegas and Saint George, Utah. In the last communication he gave his estimated time of arrival over Bryce Canyon as 12.22 p.m.

One minute before the aircraft was due over the Canyon, air traffic controllers on the ground heard the pilot's voice again. This time the message was anything but routine; he reported a fire out of control in the baggage compartment. A few moments later he reported "The tail is going out . . . we may get down and we may not."

Five minutes later another message was picked up by the helpless listeners on the ground, tersely explaining that they would try to go into "the best place". Finally there came "We may make it . . . approaching a strip."

Twenty miles to the south-west a witness who happened to glance towards the Canyon saw white

smoke and then black smoke streaming from the
aircraft. Fifteen miles from the Canyon another
witness saw that the fuselage amidships was on fire,
but thought that the stricken aircraft seemed to be
under control. Seconds later, with its lower middle
section burned out, the aircraft crashed, killing all of
the forty-six passengers and the crew of six on board.
Fire, perhaps the most dreaded danger in the air,
had claimed another victim.

A quick study of the thousands of bits of debris and
burned out sections which were strewn along an area
extending twenty-eight miles indicated that the blaze
had originated in the aircraft's belly and extended
along the right side of the fuselage where it joins the
wing. The fire was largely centred on the right sections, extending up to the top of the windows. At the
wing joint, the DC-6 carried a landing flare whose
fierce heat had severely scorched the surrounding
area. This suggested a point of origin for the fire,
although the investigators thought it more likely that
the flare had been ignited by a blaze that was already
well under way. It seemed probable that the brilliant
white light of the burning flare had attracted the
attention of witnesses on the ground.

The centre of the fire seemed to have been in a bay
colloquially known as the "boiler room", housing the
cabin heater of the air conditioning system. However,
the fire's intensity indicated that it must have been
fed by a much larger quantity of fuel flowing into the
area than would normally be supplied to the heater
unit system. The puzzle was, where did the fuel come
from?

The investigators carefully examined the construc-

Reconstructing an accident: scratch marks across line of fracture indicate that this piece of wreckage was broken *after* being hit by another object. (*Royal Aircraft Establishment*)

Water tank built for fatigue pressure tests during the investigation into the Comet accidents. (*Royal Aircraft Establishment*)

Scorched fuselage of Boeing 727 which crash-landed at Salt Lake City in November 1965. (*Associated Press Ltd.*)

Huskie crash-rescue helicopter blowing flames to one side to assist rescuers on the ground in an accident at Wilmington, North Carolina.

tion and function of the various components of the
heater system, and ordered a large number of modifications to improve its operation and safety. In addition, DC-6 operators were told to remove the landing
flares from their aircraft, as these contributed a possible
secondary danger factor. Remembering that fires on
other aircraft had been originated by the soaking of
the fuselage lining with hydraulic fluid, the investigators examined the baggage holds of the DC-6 for
evidence of hydraulic seepage. They found the baggage bay linings saturated. Although these would not
ignite easily, the CAB instructed other DC-6 operators
to examine the linings in their baggage holds, and to
remove all those which showed the least sign of
hydraulic oil contamination.

Eighteen days after the Bryce Canyon disaster,
fire broke out in another DC-6 in flight. In this
instance the crew, through swift and expert action,
managed to land the aircraft in comparative safety.
This might not have been possible if the magnesium
flares had not been removed, as instructed by the
CAB, for this prevented the fire getting completely
out of control, as it had done on the Bryce Canyon
aircraft.

The second fire nearly duplicated the first one, as
it too originated in the heater "boiler room". All
other DC-6's were grounded, while accident investigators redoubled their efforts to find out what caused
such fires to start, and to get out of control so quickly.

The first clue came during the investigation into the
second fire, when the Captain explained that the first
hint of trouble came about an hour and a half after
take-off. He had just levelled the contents of the

E

various fuel tanks by the normal method of transferring fuel from one to another, and switching the
selector valves so that each engine was drawing from
an alternate tank. After the transfer, the selector
valves were closed and the booster pumps used to
transfer the fuel were switched off.

Soon afterwards, the temperature in the passenger
cabin began to rise. At first the stewardess tried to
regulate the heat by turning the system control to
"cool". This had no effect, and she notified the
Captain. He turned the heater off. The cabin temperature, however, continued to rise, and the co-pilot,
assuming that the automatic control had gone out of
order, switched the system to manual control. At this
the cabin cooled rapidly; the stewardess asked for
more heat and, just after one o'clock, the Captain
turned the heater on again. At once the cabin temperature gauge began to rise abnormally fast, continuing to rise even when the heater was turned off
once more. By now the crew were aware that something serious was wrong.

Still climbing, the gauge registered 300°F, and a
warning light on the instrument panel came on,
indicating a fire in the "boiler room". Immediately
the Captain pressed a button releasing a dose of fire
extinguishant into the bay concerned. Before the
flame-smothering carbon dioxide could work, a smoke
detector connected to the baggage compartment
came on. At about this time the stewardess smelt an
acrid odour, and noticed smoke seeping into the
cabin.

Just before the first fire warning, the co-pilot had
noticed that the aircraft was passing Gallup and now

the pilot began a swift turning descent. While circling down, the baggage compartment smoke detector came on, and extinguishant was discharged into that area. The pilot was now struggling desperately to land the stricken aircraft. Smoke poured into the cockpit, obscuring the instruments and windscreen. To enable him to complete the landing, the co-pilot leant out of his window and talked him down, and the burning aircraft rolled to a stop.

There was little doubt that the Gallup fire closely parallelled the one over Bryce Canyon. But this time, although there had been extensive burning, the vital instruments had not been seriously harmed.

The second clue to the fire came almost by chance. While the aircraft was standing on the ramp, someone pointed out that fuel was leaking from the air-vent from the No. 3 alternate tank, and that the widening pool on the ground could catch fire. The CAB investigators agreed that the tank could be drained immediately, and its contents noted. When it was drained a peculiar thing was noted; although engine No. 3 had been drawing fuel from it for most of the trip, the tank was still full! Calculations were made of the quantity of fuel each tank should have contained after deducting the amount estimated to have been used during the flight. The final calculation of the total showed that 219 gallons of the original fuel load could not be accounted for.

The third clue was the discovery of fuel stains around the heater system's air intake scoop, located on the bottom of the fuselage. These were difficult to explain, for the nearest fuel vent was more than ten feet away, outboard, and in any case overflowing fuel would in theory vaporize and disappear harmlessly in the slipstream.

One pilot, however, wanted to satisfy himself about it by making a quick test; he painted the scoop of a DC-6 being prepared for a different set of trials with a special paint designed to discolour if contaminated with fuel. Then, in the air, the pilot repeated the fuel-levelling operation used on the Gallup aircraft, transferring fuel into the No. 3 alternate tank and allowing a small amount to overflow through the vent. After the test, he found that a trickle of fuel had washed a clean path through the paint into the air-scoop. Somehow, fuel overflowing from the vent was not vaporizing, but was being carried in the slip-stream back and sideways for a distance of more than ten feet to the scoop. The implications were only too apparent; the fuel would be sucked in and drawn to the "boiler room". Further tests proved that this was indeed what had started and sustained the two fires.

Once the cause was known, the remedy proved relatively simple. The procedure for transferring fuel was changed, and the air vents were moved outboard, nearer the wing tips and out of line with the suction airflow to the airscoop.

These fires on board the DC-6 airliners occurred in the late nineteen-forties, and caused airworthiness authorities and aircraft manufacturers to redouble their efforts to reduce the risk of fire. Today, an out-break of fire aboard a civil aircraft in flight is a rare occurrence, as the risk is minimized by careful design, much of it governed by mandatory regulations, and by rigid compliance with safety rules during proce-dures such as refuelling and defuelling.

Safety from fire is achieved first by endeavouring to ensure that one never starts, and secondly by providing means of detecting and extinguishing fires. Particular attention is paid to fireproofing the engine installation as, being hot, the engines are naturally a potential source of fires. Nacelles are designed to ensure that they are well ventilated, to prevent fuel fumes or other flammable vapours from building up into an explosive mixture. Fireproof bulkheads are installed to contain any fire that might break out, and fire extinguishant can be discharged directly into the various engine bays. A disastrous engine fire in a Convair 240 airliner at Fort Leonards Wood in August 1955, in which the crew and passengers all lost their lives, emphasized the importance of designing aircraft so that flames from an engine fire cannot readily burn backwards into a vital area; titanium or stainless steel are now used to protect vital parts of the structure. Detection of fire is particularly important in the case of engines as, once the crew is alerted, the action of shutting off the fuel supply is often all that is necessary to extinguish the fire.

Anti-fire precautions in aircraft design range from fundamental features such as the physical separation of the fuel tanks from the passenger compartments, where heating, lighting and danger in crashes might be expected, down to details such as the earthing of all pipelines to eliminate any risk from the build-up of static electricity, and the designing of fuel vents to minimize the effect of the flash from a lightning strike. At one time, to reduce the chance of a spark igniting any spilt fuel in the event of a "wheels-up" landing, inertia switches and "wipe-off" levers projecting below the fuselage were often fitted to switch off electrical power and fuel and to discharge extinguishant automatically at the moment of impact. These safety devices, however, nearly caused more disasters than they were designed to prevent, as they had a tendency sometimes to operate inadvertently. When this happened, the sudden loss of engine and electrical power was extremely serious and the discharge of extinguishant inconvenient; such devices are not now fitted.

The large quantity of flammable fuel carried on aircraft presents in itself a major fire hazard. In addition to bringing increased speed and comfort, the advent of gas-turbine powered airliners had the additional advantage of using kerosene fuel, whereas the older generation of piston-engined aircraft used petrol (gasoline). This kerosene fuel is very similar to the domestic paraffin used in the home, and is widely known as JP-1. It is also known as Avtur, Type A or Jet A fuel. It has a relatively high flash-point, and in almost all circumstances has the highest standard of safety of any aircraft fuel. For this reason it quickly became the world's standard civil jet fuel.

However, a "wide-cut" gasoline-type fuel with a relatively low flash-point, known as JP-4 (or as Avtag, Type B and Jet B fuel) is the standard fuel for land-based jet military aircraft. This is because more JP-4 than JP-1 can be obtained from a given quantity of crude oil, and in the early fifties this was considered an important factor in the event of a global war when oil resources would presumably be at a premium. This fuel is somewhat similar to domestic petrol.

A third fuel, known as JP-5 or Avcat, is used predominantly by British and American Naval Air Forces on aircraft carriers. This fuel has a higher flash-point than that of JP-1, and is therefore even safer. It is interesting to note that the special Boeing aircraft used by President Johnson for his official journeys are consistently fuelled with JP-5.

JP-4, although less safe than JP-1 because of its lower flash-point, is cheaper in some parts of the world, and it is sad to record that some airlines began to take advantage of this, using the cheaper fuel at every opportunity. One estimate indicated that this saved as much as £10,000 ($30,000) per aircraft per year.

If adopted on a world-wide scale, JP-4 promised to take away from the new generation of jet airliners the inherent safety advantage represented by their ability to run on the low volatility kerosene fuel. The trend towards the use of JP-4 started an argument on the relative safety merits of the two fuels in the early nineteen-fifties which grew into fierce public controversy in the nineteen-sixties. In September 1960, the late Lord Brabazon, the first man to hold a British Pilot's licence, issued his now famous challenge to the advocates of JP-4 to stand in a pool of JP-4 and demonstrate their faith in it by lighting a match, while he would do the same in a pool of kerosene. This challenge came to be known as the "fuel duel" but, not surprisingly, there were no takers. In November of that year Lord Brabazon, with the assistance of aircraft fire specialist John Rickard, conducted a public demonstration on British television. The pool of kerosene was ignited only with difficulty, the aid of a blow-lamp being required. The pool of JP-4 ignited at the touch of a match and flashed into flames, with explosions occurring in some of the cans from which the fuel was pouring.

On December 8, 1963, a Pan American Boeing 707 was struck by lightning and blew up while awaiting its turn to land at Philadelphia International Airport. The aircraft crashed in flames at Elkton, Maryland, after the left outer wing broke off, killing all eighty-one persons on board. Although it had been carrying kerosene, the aircraft had been refuelled with JP-4. The vapour in the tanks from the mixture of these two fuels is considered to have been within the range conducive to explosions. The CAB concluded that the probable cause of the accident was lightning-induced ignition of the fuel-air mixture in the No. 1 reserve (left wing, outer) fuel tank, with resultant explosive disintegration of the left outer wing and loss of control. In addition to the reserve tank, explosions also occurred in the wing centre tank and right reserve tank.

The Elkton accident fanned the fuel controversy anew, and the CAB recommended to the FAA that it should ban the use of JP-4 in civil aircraft. Unfortunately, the FAA did not act upon this recommendation. This attitude prevailed in spite of the evidence gathered during an official investigation conducted in 1962 by the Ministry of Aviation (now the Board of Trade), in Britain, which clearly established the greater safety of kerosene beyond all reasonable doubt. The report concluded that "on the basis of the properties of the two fuels, and especially their relative ease of ignition and rate of flame propagation, aviation kerosene is a safer fuel than JP-4 in those accidents where occupants survive the impact, and the degree

of fire risk largely determines their chance of continued survival. Such accidents mostly occur during
the landing and take-off phases. Aviation kerosene is
also safer during refuelling."

The FAA requested another investigation, this time
conducted by the Co-ordinating Research Council of
New York. At the conclusion of the year-long study
centring on a safety comparison of kerosene and
J P-4, FAA Administrator N. F. Halaby declared: "The
impartial and objective conclusions reached by this
highly specialized task force should allay any public
concern over the relative merits of jet fuels, as well as
the concern of those who claim safety superiority for
one type of jet fuel over another." This clearly contradicted the conclusion of the British report. It also
contradicted the conclusion of another American
report, produced, ironically, while the CRC investigation was still under way. This latter report, resulting
from an enquiry initiated by the Air Weather Service
(MATS) of the U.S. Air Force, concluded that "from
a purely safety point of view, it appears that kerosene
fuel should be used on all passenger flights, and on
other flights where feasible".

In view of the apparently conflicting requirements of
safety and economics, it was perhaps unfortunate that
in the CRC investigation the interests of the airlines,
oil companies and aircraft manufacturers were represented by no fewer than twenty-four people on the
committee of twenty-six. In the words of one engineer,
it was "as if the committee of the U.S. Surgeon General
investigating the relationship between smoking and
lung cancer, had been composed of tobacco growers,
cigarette manufacturers and distributors".

On November 24, 1964, while attempting to take off from Rome, a TWA Boeing 707 experienced apparent malfunctions in two engines. The pilot aborted the take-off, and then had trouble in maintaining directional control because one engine failed to develop reverse thrust. The aircraft veered off the runway and the right outer engine struck a roller. A fuel line was fractured and the fuel ignited before the aircraft came to rest. Some twenty seconds later, while the passengers were disembarking, a violent explosion occurred which killed forty-nine of the seventy-three persons on board and seriously burned many more. Reports indicated that some of the aircraft's fuel tanks, like those of the aircraft at Elkton, contained a mixture of JP-4 and kerosene, while others contained JP-4 residue and a potentially highly explosive mixture. The accident would not have been possible with kerosene, as the vapour-air mixture would have been too weak to explode.

This catastrophe at Rome added further impetus to the campaign of John Rickard with the newly formed Air Safety Group in Britain, and of associations such as the Airways Club (now the Airline Passengers Association) of New York, against the general use of JP-4. Success came in January 1965, when Pan American World Airways publicly announced that it would in future use kerosene "wherever possible". The airline statement indicated that its decision was influenced most by the Airways Club campaign, and made it clear that it was acting reluctantly in minimizing its use of JP-4 fuel. "The public has been educated to mistrust JP-4," Pan American said. "Pan American believes, as does the FAA, that on the basis of present information there is no justification for the mistrust." Soon afterwards Trans World Airlines, influenced by the public pressure against J P-4 and Pan American's decision, followed suit. An intra-company communique was issued stating that "commencing immediately, we will suspend the use of J P-4 in TWA jets except where kerosene is not available, or where other pressing circumstances require the use of J P-4".

In Britain, the use of J P-4 is not banned officially, although aircraft must be cleared by the Air Registration Board before this fuel can be used. The ARB, however, endeavours to persuade operators on the British Register to use kerosene only, except where it is necessary to refuel at an airfield where kerosene is not available. To date British operators appear to have accepted this persuasion. No British operator uses J P-4 regularly. Australia has outlawed the use of J P-4, and its Department of Civil Aviation is to be congratulated on being the only airworthiness authority which has squarely faced its public responsibility in this matter.

When this book closed for press a number of airlines were still using J P-4 regularly.

In final comment on the fuel controversy, the fence-sitting attitude of the International Air Transport Association is quite incomprehensible. Worse, the Association is on record as stating "that both kerosene and J P-4 are fully acceptable for airline use". This is surprising from an association which, as its one-time director-general Sir William Hildred often said, is concerned first and foremost with air safety. Unlike a criminal, J P-4 should be considered guilty until proved innocent.

The general hazard represented by lightning strikes is fairly small. Aircraft are, in fact, hit by lightning relatively infrequently, about once every 2,500 flying hours in the case of piston-engined aircraft and once every 10,000 hours in the case of the higher-flying jet aircraft. The damage is usually slight, the only known instances where a lightning strike had serious consequences being the Elkton Boeing 707, and a TWA Constellation lost near Milan in 1959, which suffered an explosion in an almost empty fuel tank. In military aircraft, there have been a number of cases of tip tanks containing J P-4 being exploded by lightning. So far as is known, there has not been a single case of a kerosene explosion in normal flight.

Although for obvious reasons aircraft engine fuel presents the greatest potential fire hazard, considerable attention has also been given to the development of a lubricating fluid with a high flash-point for hydraulic systems. Relatively small amounts of hydraulic fluid are carried on board aircraft, but it operates under high pressure and in the event of a leak can atomize in a fine spray. Early hydraulic fluids had a low flash-point and when heated they tended to give off dense smoke if not toxic fumes. Typical of the early hydraulic fires was the one which occurred in a BEA Viscount at London Airport in January 1960. The accident occurred on landing in conditions of fog; after the aircraft had crossed the end of the runway, it ran into an area of much reduced visibility. The Captain lost the visual references needed to judge the flare out and the nosewheel struck the runway heavily. The leg collapsed and the aircraft then travelled for a distance of 500 yards on the mainwheels with its nose rubbing on the runway before it came to rest. Immediately the aircraft began to fill with smoke, but all the crew and passengers were quickly and safely evacuated.

When the aircraft's noseleg collapsed, it fractured the main hydraulic pipe feeding the steering jacks. Hydraulic oil at a high temperature and pressure was then released in the form of a spray on to the tyres and surrounding structure, and probably on to some of the baggage in the front freight hold. This hydraulic mist was then ignited, it is thought, by the frictional heat of the leg scraping along the runway. Because all the doors and two rear emergency exits were open, and because of the hole made in the underside by the nosewheels, a chimney effect was produced in the fuselage which rapidly intensified the fire and accelerated its course rearwards. A fierce fire developed which burnt through the top of the fuselage and spread back as far as the tail unit, almost completely destroying the fuselage. In this instance, although no lives were lost, the use of an inflammable hydraulic fluid was responsible for the "writing off" of a valuable aircraft.

Inflammable hydraulic fluid also played its part in the Swissair Caravelle crash at Zurich in September 1963, in which all eighty occupants lost their lives; this was the first major disaster suffered by Swissair in its thirty-two year history. Having taxied to the take-off point, the Captain was advised by the control tower that the visibility was below the minimum requirements. He made a dummy run with the dual objective of assessing the conditions and of dispersing fog by his jet efflux. The aircraft took off after about thirteen minutes of manoeuvring on the ground, and crashed eight minutes later. The extensive ground taxiing had overheated the brakes; the heat from the brakes weakened the wheels, and a wheel rim failed, bursting a tyre. The burst tyre fractured a hydraulic line and fluid sprayed on to the hot brakes. The fluid caught fire and at least one of the wheels was burning at some point during the take-off, probably just after the aircraft left the ground.

What happened next is conjectural, but there is little doubt that burning hydraulic fluid did play a part. It seems that after take-off another tyre burst in the landing gear bay. Whether this explosion was assisted by the burning hydraulic fluid, or whether it would have occurred anyway due to the brake heat soak-back into the wheels is not known. This second tyre failure damaged adjacent fuel lines, spraying fuel on to the still extremely hot brakes. A major fire started, spread rapidly back along the fuselage and reached the tail unit. Parts of this were burnt away, causing loss of control.

After this accident Swissair fitted blow-out fuses to the wheels of their Caravelle fleet. These consist of metal plugs with a low melting point, which fuse before the wheel itself weakens to permit air from the tyre to escape safely. In addition, Swissair fitted protective metal shields over vital hydraulic and fuel lines in the landing gear bays. The accident emphasized that safety in aviation is often a chain consisting of many links. The strength of the chain depends upon the strength of the weakest link, and inflammable hydraulic fluid had been shown to be a weak link. On current aircraft, failure of this particular link is prevented by the use of a chemically fire-resistant hydraulic fluid known as Skydrol. This fluid was invented by Douglas in the early fifties, and has been further developed in close co-operation with Monsanto.

The general risk of a fire occurring in an airliner in flight today is very low, owing to the precautions taken and care devoted to the problem in the design stage, and the extensive testing during the initial certification programme. Most airlines, in fact, seem to be worried more by the number of false fire warnings reported than with cases involving a genuine fire!

Much, however, remains to be done to reduce the hazard of fire on the ground after a crash. That even experienced manufacturers can be caught out was made evident by the tragic accident to a United Airlines Boeing 727 at Salt Lake City in November 1965. Coming in to land at the City Airport, the airliner touched down heavily some 200 feet short of the runway. The landing gear collapsed and the stricken aircraft skidded along the ground and burst into flames. A woman passenger forced open an emergency door and escaped to safety, followed by fifty other people, including the crew of six. Unfortunately, forty-one others in the rear of the aircraft who had survived the actual landing perished in the fierce asphyxiating fire, as they pushed frantically to the exits. CAB investigators probing the wreckage commented on the ferocity of the fire, due in part to the use of combustible materials to furnish the cabin.

After the Salt Lake City accident, a close look was taken at the "crash worthiness" of the 727 and other aircraft, to see if they were as good as they could be. In the case of the 727, the examination resulted in several changes designed to re-route fuel lines and hydraulic pipes away from the landing gear. In the event of a landing heavy enough to cause damage, the landing gear should now "fail clean", and not rupture the fuel tanks, or the fuel or hydraulic lines.

It has been estimated that the number of deaths in crashes could be reduced by 7 to 15 per cent if the aircraft could be prevented from catching fire or exploding after coming to rest. The general problem is being actively investigated by the airlines, the military, by the FAA, CAB, NASA and many other bodies.

A first easy step towards reducing the crash fire risk is to standardize on kerosene as the fuel for normal airline use. Not only is kerosene vapour generally too weak to explode; the relatively slow rate at which fire spreads across spilt kerosene provides a few extra seconds which can make the difference between life and death for passengers and crew. The universal use of kerosene would not, of course, eliminate the crash fire risk completely; it would merely reduce it or prevent the death rate from increasing, as would result from a wholesale swing to J P-4.

Much of the fuel, whether kerosene or J P-4, released during a crash may be dispersed, sometimes producing a mist of highly combustible vapours. The rate of vaporization could be significantly reduced by the development of a gelled fuel, of high viscosity or "solid". In the solid state, flame propagation rates are reduced about 97 per cent and flame durations are reduced about 85 per cent. Also, leakage from rup- tured tanks is all but eliminated. It may be possible to develop a gel fuel which would remain in the liquid

A sequence of three photographs showing the Boeing 707 prototype, fitted with blown flaps, landing at the same low speed as a lightweight twin-engined Beechcraft.

New developments in passenger aircraft: mock-up of the Boeing 747 main passenger cabin.

A blown lift rotor developed by Britain's National Gas Turbine Establishment. (*National Gas Turbine Establishment*)

state during normal operations, but which would become solid under crash impact loads.

Most current airliners have integral fuel tanks; the fuel is carried in the wing in the sealed spaces formed by the wing skins, front and rear spars and the wing ribs. A return to the bag tanks used in the old generation of piston-engined airliners may be foreshadowed by recent Pentagon and FAA tests with "tough wall" tanks made of nylon and polyurethene. Carrying one such tank, a helicopter was deliberately crashed into a jagged rock at high speed; the crash only caused a one-eighth inch crack.

Investigations are also under way into the development of a special high-expansion fog or foam which could be released to fill the fuselage after a crash, increasing the time available for evacuation under severe fire conditions. Both these developments, and others, would involve weight penalties and, in the case of a reversion to flexible bag fuel tanks, a loss of volume of fuel. No single operator or aircraft manufacturer could consider adopting such a safety feature while competitors considered the economic price too high for the return in increased safety.

NASA in the early fifties developed an inertia-switch operated system that at the moment of impact directed a powerful stream of water on to key hot areas of the engines, to prevent any fuel spilt from being ignited by contact with those parts of the engine. The system was demonstrated in twenty simulated crashes using surplus World War II aircraft, not one of which resulted in a fire. However, such a system has not been developed for use on airliners, partly because the weight would take about 800 pounds away from

F

the payload, partly because of the difficulty of preventing inadvertent operation in the air, and partly because the risk of ignition from friction sparks and electrical arcing would still remain as would the tank explosion risk.

Another possible line of development is the rapid tackling of aircraft fires by ground services. The U.S. Air Force, for example, maintains a fleet of nearly a hundred crash-rescue helicopters specially equipped to combat fires. Their value was dramatically demonstrated when a C-123 transport crashed and burst into flames at an air show in Wilmington, North Carolina. When the crash occurred the crew of an Air Force Kaman Huskie crash-rescue helicopter were sitting outside their aircraft, which was on show. Within two minutes the crew had pushed the helicopter out of the display area and were airborne, on their way to the crash scene.

As the helicopter hovered over the nose of the burning craft, the downwash from the rotor blew through the broken windscreen and along the fuselage, keeping it clear of smoke, heat and flames. Rescue personnel worked for ten minutes freeing victims trapped in the cockpit and up to fifteen minutes in the mid-section of the fuselage. At one point the helicopter landed to discharge a flight surgeon. In that brief moment smoke billowed through the stricken aircraft, overcoming a fireman working in the rear of the fuselage. Moments later the helicopter was airborne, again driving fresh air through the crash wreckage. The fireman who had been overcome reported that he could feel the blast of clean air sweep the fuselage free of choking smoke and heat. When its

fire suppression job was over, the Huskie flew three
critically injured survivors to a near-by hospital,
making a vertical descent, with the rotors clearing the
side of the building by six to eight feet, on to one half
of a tennis court.

As far as is known, no such helicopters serve at any
civil airport.

10

Murphy's Law

The prototype Avro Tudor II, a development of Britain's first attempt at producing a large four-engined civil airliner after the 1939–45 war, stood ready for flight. It had just spent a period on the ground during which the incidence of the tailplane had been altered and the stiffness of the elevator control circuit increased. The four Rolls-Royce Merlin 600 Special engines were run and proved satisfactory, after which the aircraft was refuelled.

At 10.40 a.m. on August 23, 1947, the flight crew boarded the aircraft. These included the company's Chief Test Pilot, S. A. Thorn, a man of great experience, and Roy Chadwick, c.b.e., Chief Designer of the aircraft, who was on the test flight as an interested observer.

The aircraft took off normally after a run of approximately 800 yards. As it was flying level down the latter part of the runway, at a height of about fifty feet, the starboard wing started to drop. The wing tip hit the ground about fifteen yards in front of an eight-foot wire fence which marked the boundary of the airfield; it scraped through the fence leaving a gap several yards wide. After a short break, the mark, this time more pronounced and deeper, reappeared on the other side of the fence, continuing for several yards until the wing struck the corner of a hedge surrounding an adjacent orchard. This impact caused the wing tip to telescope and break away from the outer wing, followed by a portion of the aileron. The aircraft continued in a steeply banked attitude, scraping its wing along the ground, shedding large pieces of skin, formers and spar booms. Finally, when most of the outer wing had been ripped off, the nose of the aircraft ploughed into the ground, and the tail reared up as the machine slithered on its nose down a slope towards a pond surrounded by a belt of oak trees. The stricken aircraft crashed into the trees and ploughed into the pond. The two pilots, trapped in the nose of the aircraft, were drowned, and Mr. Chadwick was killed instantly.

This sad crash was very definitely an accident which should never have happened. When the wreckage was recovered and examined, the aileron chains in both control columns were found incorrectly assembled, resulting in the ailerons working in the reverse sense. The aileron handgrip rotated a sprocket inside the control column; a chain passed over this sprocket and down the inside of the control column where it was attached to two cables. In this aircraft the chain had been crossed inside the arm of the column, so that it was connected to the wrong cable. Movement of the aileron handgrip therefore produced the opposite result from the one intended.

The pilot, concentrating his attention during take-off on the attitude of the aircraft, did not really have a chance. He must have thought that the aircraft had encountered a gust of wind, causing the wing to drop. His response would have been instinctive and, when the right wing continued to drop as he put the control over to the left, the compulsive reaction must have been to put the stick over more and more. He probably never realized exactly what had happened.

This crash provided tragic proof of Murphy's Law: "If a part can be installed incorrectly, someone, someday, will install it that way." In everyday life, the consequences of Murphy's Law are rarely dangerous, the vacuum cleaner that blows dirt out instead of sucking it in being merely frustrating. However, realizing its possible serious consequences in the field of aviation, designers go to great lengths to ensure that, wherever possible, things can only be done one way. In fact, it is mandatory that certain key features of aircraft be designed this way, and perhaps the real tragedy of the Tudor accident was that the possibility of crossing the flying controls had been foreseen.

It was not the first aircraft to have its aileron controls reversed. During the trials for the 1927 Schneider Trophy contest, a British seaplane, the Bristow Crusader, had taken off and instantly started to turn. The turn steepened, went over the vertical, merged into a dive, and the aircraft went down into the waters of the Lagoon in a great spout of water. The pilot miraculously survived, and said he thought that "something had gone wrong with the controls". When the wreckage was recovered and inspected, it was found that the aileron control runs had been incorrectly connected, so that movement of the control column produced the opposite of the desired effect.

Control runs must now be designed in such a way that it is mechanically impossible for them to be connected incorrectly; the simplest method is to have different sizes of end fittings for connecting the two control cables. Had this been done the Tudor would not have crashed.

Another component which demonstrated Murphy's Law was the non-return or check valve, which is designed to permit the flow of air, fuel or other fluid in one direction only. It was not long before one was installed the wrong way round, so that it *stopped* fluid flowing in the required direction. To prevent this happening, such valves are now made with inlet and outlet connectors of different sizes or types so that it is impossible to install them incorrectly. On some valves with the new ends, however, Murphy's Law still operated. It was possible to assemble the internal seat, ball and spring back-to-front in the body, so that even though the complete valve was installed correctly, it permitted fluid to flow in the wrong direction owing to the incorrect assembly of the internal parts. The problem was finally solved by designing the internal parts so that they too could only be assembled one way.

Occasionally Murphy's Law results in laughter instead of tragedy. One maintenance engineer recalls that a few years ago the pride of his company was a transonic jet fighter. Although not delivered in large production quantities, it was a significant breakthrough in many respects. One of these machines, used for flight test purposes, was in the hangar for about two months while some design changes were installed. Finally the changes were completed, and the great day came when the aeroplane was towed outside for its first engine run. After the engine had started, the pilot tried out the brakes – and hydraulic fluid squirted from the pitot head!

As indicated by the non-return valves, it is not always easy to "design out" the Murphy-factor in aircraft. One aeroplane incorporates a wing fuel tank pressure regulator, which regulates pressure in the tank by comparing it with the outside air pressure. There were two connections on the regulator, one reading tank pressure and the other outside air pressure. On the original design the pipelines leading to the connections ran parallel for some distance, making it quite easy to fix a pipe to the wrong connection. In fact, there was a fifty-fifty chance of the pipe being attached to the wrong connection, and this was about the rate at which incorrect connections were made. After several serious incidents, one of the connections was changed to a different size, so that it was impossible to connect the wrong pipe. Only the connection was changed, while the threaded holes in the body remained unaltered.

However, when the regulators were removed for overhaul, the two connections were removed from the old regulator and fitted to the new regulator about to be installed in the aircraft. Once again there was a fifty-fifty chance of a connection being screwed into the wrong position, and again it happened. The instrument manufacturer was urgently requested to re-design the regulator so that it had different sized holes for the two connections. The piping on the aircraft was modified in expectation. Unfortunately, the new regulators were not immediately available, and to enable existing stocks to be used, the design provided a reducing union so that the new piping could be attached to the old regulator. In the interim period before the new regulators arrived, the pipes were connected incorrectly at least once; somebody arrived with a pocket-full of adaptors to ensure that the lines could be crossed. Only with the advent of the fully modified regulator was the problem finally eliminated.

That is, it was solved at the regulator end. The pipeline reading the outside air pressure ended in a simple union protruding through the bulkhead in a wheel-well. With commendable foresight, somebody had looked at the union and thought "Somebody is going to see this union and put a blanking cap on it." To remove the Murphy-factor, a guard was fitted over the union. Nevertheless, somebody looked under the guard, thought someone had forgotten to fit a cap, and fitted one. The simple open union has now been changed for a specially designed end fitting which really is considered to be Murphy-Law-proof.

When a new aeroplane is being designed, teams of specialists pore over the drawings to try and ensure that the various systems and fitting assemblies are Murphy-proof as far as is practical. In addition to the mandatory items such as pipelines and cable connections, less obvious components such as bell-cranks are examined to see whether they can be installed incorrectly so that either the mechanical advantage is changed, or the linkage goes over dead centre. Further experience is gained while the new aircraft is being built and during the period of intensive development that follows the first flight until it is certificated and ready for service.

With aircraft in service, the Murphy-factor is kept at bay by programmes of training for the various maintenance procedures. Finally, a strictly-controlled system of inspection and quality assurance makes certain that any work done is properly checked and any examples of Murphy's Law uncovered and rectified before any harm is done.

To safer flying

"Air accidents kill 20,000 in a year." This startling headline could become fact by the end of the century, according to Dr Lundberg, head of Sweden's Aeronautical Research Institute and a world authority on aviation safety. This prediction of fatalities is not based upon the assumption that air travel is going to become more dangerous in thirty years time. It is the figure that will result if the current rate of aviation growth continues and the present accident rate remains constant; it will be due solely to the increased numbers of aeroplanes that will be flying in the future.

However, the present "low" rate of accidents (about one passenger killed per 200 million passenger miles) kills enough people annually to create passenger anxiety. Every accident involving an airliner sends a chill of fear through the millions who have flown and through those about to travel by air. Each accident induces a number of potential air travellers to make a vow never to fly. A total of fatalities as high as that estimated by Lundberg would tend to curtail the growth of air transport or even reverse it, because of the publicity and public fear. There will certainly be intense public concern at future accidents involving the 250-seat airbuses and 500-seat jumbo jets which, in a single mid-air collision, could kill a thousand people.

The accident rate must come down in the future, and it must come down more rapidly than annual airline growth. Dr. Lundberg suggests that to be acceptable, the risk must be reduced to one-twentieth or so of its present level. This would mean a "target" of no more than 300 to 400 air deaths a year at the end of the century.

Some readers may think it strange to consider even 400 deaths (half the present number) as tolerable; they may assert that the only acceptable accident rate is perfect safety. This ideal objective, however, is impracticable, as it would prevent the compromises without which no aeroplane could fly. For example, the pilot of a pressurized airliner should be provided with hemispheric vision from the cockpit to reduce the collision potential. However, a "wrap-around" type of windshield would increase the hazards of a bird strike and of explosive decompression, would create discomfort from sun glare and would make it impossible to provide the space necessary for essential controls and instrumentation. A compromise is necessary to accommodate all these factors, making perfect safety impossible.

How will safer flying be achieved? Although it must depend on a combination of many factors, the following question was put to a number of the world's leading airworthiness authorities and organizations specializing in air safety, as a possible means of finding out:

"Which single aid, device, regulation, procedure or development do you think would contribute most effectively to an increase in the standard of world-wide air safety? The device or regulation can be either existing or one not yet developed."

One of the early replies came from the FAA, who commented that the question was certainly a most provocative one, and most difficult to answer objectively. FAA goals in air safety are directed towards consideration of an aviation system rather than of any single device, as well as the relationship between the parts of that system, which include the aircraft, airmen, airports, navigation and communications, aeronautical and weather information, rules and procedures, and air traffic control. Equally important are pilot operating procedures and pilot education and training.

Having considered the matter in these official overall terms, the FAA began to be more specific. In the opinion of some FAA experts, the greatest single contribution to air safety would be the development of an effective, reliable anti-collision device which could take the form either of ground radar capable of generating altitude information for the use of ground controllers, or an airborne warning and advisory device for direct use on the flight deck.

This suggestion was corroborated by the British Air Line Pilots Association who, after commenting that air safety depends upon everything "from the pilot's sun glasses to the length of the runway", stated: "If pushed to provide one answer, an efficient proximity warning device would be an invaluable aid in the future years, as the traffic density in the air will be ever increasing."

The overwhelming majority of the 400 or so mid-air collisions over the past twenty-five years have occurred, rather surprisingly, in daylight and good weather, most of them while one or both of the aircraft were preparing to land, or in an airport traffic pattern. Only thirty of the collisions, involving airliners, accounted for more than half of the fatalities resulting from all the collisions. Thus, equipment which would aid in the avoidance of collisions of light aircraft would have more effect upon the total number of collisions, while equipment for airliners would be important in reducing the death toll. This will be even truer in the days of the jumbo-jet airliners.

What is needed is a simple and reliable device which would first warn an aircraft when it is in danger of colliding with another aircraft, and then indicate the appropriate action for avoiding the collision. To be fully effective, the device should work in all weathers, which means that it will probably have to be some kind of radar equipment. Unfortunately, equipment of the size and power that could reasonably be installed in airliners would have neither the range to be effective, nor the ability to distinguish a safe miss distance course from a collision course.

Experts feel that the most accurate quantity available on which to base evasive manoeuvres is the local barometric pressure. In theory this information could be interchanged between aircraft, and a collision avoided by the higher aircraft climbing, and the lower aircraft descending, enough to achieve a safe vertical separation. Unfortunately, in practice such a system would be plagued by false alarms, resulting in an aircraft being forced to climb or descend to avoid another whose course would never bring it within miles of a collision. The number of false alarms can be reduced by the use of more complex and expensive equipment. Both aircraft would need to be equipped, and the utility of the envisaged equipment is further reduced by the fact that for the warnings to be of any value, the aircraft must be flying on essentially straight courses at the time measurements are made. Thus such equipment would be of little use in terminal areas where the majority of serious collisions occur.

Although the problem seems insoluble, development work is proceeding on experimental equipment approaching the matter from different angles. One device under development is the McDonnell Collision Avoidance System. If an aircraft is on a collision course, the pilot is warned aurally, directing his attention to an "Eros" indicator which tells him to climb, descend or fly level. This system is said to have a range of up to 150 miles, to accommodate up to 1,000 aircraft and to provide a sixty-second warning for aircraft closing at speeds of up to four times the speed of sound.

Less complex would be the development of a proximity warning indicator, which would merely tell the pilot where to look. Such indicators would be useful particularly in light aircraft, since a large proportion of the collisions occur at low closing speeds, where ample time for evasive action would have been available had either pilot seen the other aircraft. Experiments have been made with infra-red, optical and ultra-violet phenomena, but nothing has yet reached the operational stage.

A practical start on this difficult problem has, however, been made by the FAA; it comprises a series of tests to determine whether radar pictures transmitted from the ground to a television receiver in an aircraft can help pilots to avoid collisions and bad weather, and whether they can be used as a navigational aid. Sixteen pilots were used in the test; eight of these, from the FAA, were experienced in interpreting radar displays, and eight, from general aviation, had little or no experience. The pictures, of radar screens being used by FAA air-traffic controllers, covered a thirty-mile radius and were received on a 5-inch television screen installed in the flight compartment. The results are currently being analysed.

A second body of technicians in the FAA maintains that the best answer to improved air safety lies in improved aircraft crashworthiness. In this connection many people believe that the successful development of a gelled fuel could be the best means of saving lives in survivable crashes. If fires could be prevented, this alone would reduce fatalities by over half.

The crashworthiness of airliners, an old and difficult problem, is indeed worth closer attention. More people survive in air crashes than is generally realized, and if some passengers survive why not most or all of them? The importance of incorporating fundamental crashworthiness features in the basic design of airliners was tragically underlined during the accident of a Boeing 727 at Salt Lake City, in November 1965. The heavy touchdown damaged the landing gear which in turn fractured adjacent fuel and electrical lines, allowing the escaping fuel to ignite. The flames spread to the cabin where the furnishings, although basically fire-proof, generated thick black toxic fumes which over-came many of the unhurt passengers as they scrambled for the exits.

As a direct result of this accident the FAA reviewed the crashworthiness of all other passenger-carrying aircraft operating in the United States, with particular regard to the consequences of failure of the landing gear and attachment structures, the relative disposi-tion of the fuel and electrical lines and the possibility of interaction in the event of rupture of the fuel lines and damage to the electrical cables, and the resistance of the cabin furnishings to burning and the release of toxic fumes. These points will be borne in mind in the design of future airliners, as well as other small and quite inexpensive improvements, such as the proper sinking of food trays.

Closely allied to crashworthiness is the provision of survival equipment. In general, aircraft survival equipment compares unfavourably with that available in shipping disasters, although sea travel has a far better record of safety. The International Federation of Air Line Pilots Associations recommends that life-jackets should be carried on all civil aircraft, as even on a route entirely over land, an aircraft may be compelled to ditch, possibly on a river or lake. In addition, all cushions, blankets and seat covers, possessing no inherent buoyancy, can be made to hold air, and means are available to treat fibrous materials to make them buoyant. Buoyant ropes have been used at sea for twenty-five years. Finally, the IFALPA recommends that life-rafts for all persons on board should be carried on all aircraft flying over water at any stage of the flight, including take-off and landing. This recommendation is strongly endorsed by B. W. Townshend, who has made a life-long study of ditchings and survival problems, and by the Australian Air Line Pilots Association who, referring to the non-carriage of life-rafts on certain over-water routes, said that they could not explain to passengers being eaten by sharks that "it should not have happened, on the basis of statistics".

Careful consideration must also be given to the location of life-raft stowages, which should be determined in the initial design stages and not added as an afterthought. The mere provision of life-rafts does not automatically ensure safety, as indicated by the accident in August 1962 to a DC-8 which slewed off the runway into adjacent water while taking off from Galeao airport. Nobody was injured, but although both life-jackets and life-rafts were carried, fourteen of the ninety-four passengers and one crew member subsequently drowned.

Life-rafts should be installed so that they can be launched immediately, without requiring manhandling or movement from one part of an aircraft to another. The launching mechanism should be simple, to eliminate any risk of premature release. Life-raft stowage in the wing is not necessarily the best place for all aircraft; the loss of a wing has on at least one occasion caused the loss of all life-rafts on that side.

The relative safety of rearward-facing seats should also be investigated internationally. If the evidence indicates that they definitely increase the chance of survival in many types of crash landings, they should be adopted universally. In a statement of policy on this subject in 1959, the British Government admitted that rearward-facing seats were safer; in fact, it requires such seating on British aircraft used for trooping. Opposition to rearward-facing seating seems to be based on the assumption that it would somehow lose business, and that it would cost extra money. A loss of revenue has never been conclusively proved and many estimates of the cost involved, mainly in strengthening the floor, are considered wildly pessimistic. On commercial aircraft previously used for carrying troops, where it was uneconomical to change the seats around, the only passenger reactions noted were that some travellers stated that it was the first aircraft they had travelled in which they "flew backwards", and that passengers trying to get the quietest seats tended to walk forward to the noisiest ones, being misled by the direction in which the seats were facing! As for the extra cost, no doubt the fifty-nine passengers killed in the Lockheed Electra which crash-landed at Boston in October 1960 would have considered the slight "premium" involved well worth-while, as experts consider they would have survived had they been in rearward-facing seats.

The problem of aircraft flying into mountains will need serious attention before the advent of the airbuses and jumbo-jets. Perhaps with this in mind, the secretary of Britain's Flight Safety Committee suggested a "ground proximity warning device" as his personal idea of the best single contribution to safer flying. A similar suggestion was made by J. A. Derbyshire, an aviation insurance claims specialist, who commented:

"It would seem that a great many accidents have been caused in the past by pilots descending into high ground under the mistaken impression that they have already passed over it. Therefore, we think that a useful development would be a highly accurate ground surveillance radar which also displayed right alongside the radarscope information from a radio altimeter and a DME (Distance Measuring Equipment)."

In connection with this general problem, the present unsatisfactory state of aircraft charts should be investigated. Many pilots complain that existing charts give inadequate and misleading terrain height information. It seems common sense that these charts should have a simplified but useful presentation of the height of terrain by contours. The contours suggested would be much simpler than those on current topographical charts; adequate information can be presented to air crew without unnecessary details. This matter does not require a major technological breakthrough, nor the expenditure of vast sums of money. It is something that can and should be done now.

The Flight Safety Foundation and its stable partner, the Cornell-Guggenheim Aviation Safety Center, have firm ideas on the subject of increased safety. Air safety "breakthroughs", explained Harry Guggenheim, chairman of the Foundation Committee of the Safety Center "are not easily come by, but there are at least three areas where major progress might be made – progress of such importance as to reduce fatalities significantly." The first of these concerned "the suppressing of fire in the event of a crash".

A second area where the Safety Center considers a

breakthrough possible is "in withholding licenses for new aircraft until they have been thoroughly proven airworthy. We should not take for granted in the future that whenever a new aeroplane is put into service the public should be exposed, as in the past, to a number of fatal accidents before flaws are corrected and safety of operation assured. The process of certificating aircraft for airworthiness should not have serious weaknesses which only time will expose.

"The public should not be permitted to fly in new models until crews have been trained to perfection in flying them under all flying conditions."

Thirdly, the Center suggested that "a suitable monitoring system should be used to detect and warn of departures from good safety practices before they end in accidents. Such monitoring systems must not be used for 'policing', since this would lead only to resentment and might actually reduce the effectiveness of the warnings. Rather, a suitable monitoring system should elicit the active co-operation and interest of pilot and crew. Its purpose should be to prevent, not punish."

This suggestion is a valuable possibility, if the co-operation of pilots can be obtained. It is considered in some quarters that had such a system been in use, the three or four approach accidents which marred the large-scale introduction into service of the Boeing 727 airliner might well have been prevented. The flight recorders now fitted to all large transport aircraft provide the basis from which a suitable monitoring system could be evolved. These three suggestions were warmly endorsed by Jerome Lederer of the Flight Safety Foundation.

The Civil Aeronautics Board, like many of the organizations approached, pointed out that "there is no single answer", continuing: "We could certainly develop a rather lengthy list of items which could make significant contributions. For example, on a domestic basis, it is considered that when the time arrives, hopefully in the not too distant future, that there is 100 per cent air traffic control radar coverage at both upper and lower levels, there will then be a tool to be utilized for the development of positive control coast-to-coast. Another item which occurs to us is that if and when our National Meteorological Authority develops a means for producing weather forecasts of 100 per cent accuracy, that most assuredly would be a major contribution.

"We do not mention these two items with the idea that they are considered at the top of our hypothetical list. We merely mention them as examples of two of the many items which could and perhaps some day will contribute to air safety."

The CAB reference to improved air traffic control was echoed by Britain's Guild of Air Pilots and Air Navigators (GAPAN) who commented:

"Members of the Guild believe that the single most effective step which would lead to an increase in safety standards internationally would be the institution of controlled air space in which all aviation operations, civil and military, would take place. This automatically implies the provision of all the necessary facilities, including navigation aids and all the essential equipment for air traffic control, such as adequate communications facilities and radar.

"General aviation enthusiasts might interpret this

as meaning that the Guild wishes to see their activities curtailed. This is not the case since we believe that complete control of airspace would result in more freedom than exists, for example in Western Europe and the United Kingdom, because collision risk would be considerably reduced and the practice of sterilizing large areas of airspace for occasional specific activity would be eliminated.

"In another aspect, one of the most necessary requirements is an accurate altimeter for use at all flight levels; the lack of it was one of the main reasons for the pilots' objections voiced strongly in 1965 to the proposed reduction in vertical clearance over the North Atlantic to 1,000 feet.

"Since the most dangerous phases of flight are the landing and take-off, a very pressing need is to maintain at all times the facilities to aid these operations; in other words, airfields should be fully equipped technically today for the operation of large turbo-jet aircraft; by the time the supersonic transport is introduced any necessary modifications for its safe operation should have been made."

It is quite terrifying to think that pilots have not yet been provided with foolproof instruments. Among those that need improving, in addition to the altimeters and engine speed indicators already mentioned, are airspeed indicators. Even this most fundamental of instruments can be misread by trained pilots. In 1966 British European Airways carried out a comprehensive evaluation of four different types of a.s.i's, and discovered that out of 3,840 readings, 153 were gross errors (that is, more than seven knots from the correct reading), and that errors of *at least* 100 *knots* had been made on each of the indicators under test!

The point about airfields made by GAPAN was emphasized by America's ALPA, who commented: "You'll probably find our opinion rather prosaic, but it is the Air Line Pilot's Association's belief that the greatest contribution which could be made to air safety would be operational improvements in the airport and terminal area where the greatest number of accidents occur." This belief has been backed up by a formidable collection of evidence and data recently submitted to a committee in the United States Senate. Not all the suggested improvements require vast sums of money on research. The ALPA report cites instances of runway signs mounted on massive I-section steel posts embedded in projecting concrete footings, of boulders from previous construction work left lying along the edge of a runway, of thick concrete manhole covers near runways, and of runways with a sharp drop-off to a soft shoulder. All these spell trouble for an airliner that inadvertently leaves the runway, which is not an uncommon occurrence. Too many airfields still proudly mount their array of approach lights on top of sturdy poles. These are guaranteed to do as much damage to an airliner flying a little too low as their counterparts erected in open fields in the 1939-45 war to prevent enemy troop-carrying aircraft from landing!

One way of attempting to answer the question is to ask where the majority of accidents occur. It does not take long to discover this; about half of the jet airliner mishaps have occurred during the landing phase. The individual accidents have been due to a variety of detail causes: pilots striking the sea or ground while believing themselves to be higher, pilots misreading instruments, pilots reading the wrong instrument, the incorrect interpretation of landmarks, and the false identification of airfields and runways. The fundamental cause, however, is the same in every case: the pilot's inability to determine his exact position in the air relative to the ground. Most of the accidents would have been prevented if there had been some form of reliable pictorial navigation display. Australia's Department of Civil Aviation suggested: "It is our view that perhaps the most effective single contribution that could be made to world aviation safety is the development of a device which will reliably and accurately indicate to the pilot the position of his aircraft in relation to the surface of the earth at all times and in all conditions. The most appealing method of satisfying this requirement is some form of pictorial cockpit presentation. This has already been achieved, to some degree, with Decca, and other devices are under development in the United States utilizing VOR and DME to supply the basic information.

"Currently all these aids suffer from some form of limitation but future technical developments may provide the increased accuracy, reliability and economy necessary to produce equipment suitable for general use."

The Society of Licensed Aircraft Engineers and Technologists (SLAET) in Britain, after considering the question at two meetings, put forward no less than four suggestions: a universally accepted mandatory approach pattern and landing procedure with standardized equipment, a computer-programmed integrated flight system which would be pilot-monitored,

an infallible vertical take-off and landing system, and
the use of aircraft limited to landing speeds not greater
than sixty knots.

Apart from the pilots concerned, few people are
aware of the wide variations of approach and landing
procedures throughout the world, or of the extremely
limited aids that exist away from the major airports.
The first of SLAET's four points is strongly under-
written by Roy Broadbent who, as Deputy Director
of the Ministry of Aviation (now part of the Board
of Trade), suggested the universal adoption of VASI,
a device mounted at the side of the runway which lets
a pilot know if he is on the correct approach path, or
if he is undershooting or overshooting. VASI (Visual
Approach Slope Indicator) was invented at the Royal
Aircraft Establishment (RAE) in Great Britain. It
consists of a frangible box containing a number of
lamps similar to the sealed-beam units used in motor
cars, a simple coloured glass assembly and a slot in
the end opposite the lamps. This simple optical system,
without lenses or moving parts, produces a pattern of
lights to guide the pilot. If he is on the desired glide-
path a red light on white is visible; if he is too low,
both sets of lights are red, and if too high, both lights
are white. The RAE lighting system was adopted as a
world standard by ICAO in 1961 for runways used by
aircraft whose speed or rate of descent are such that
the approach path must be maintained within fine
limits, or if the pilot has inadequate visual references
or hazards to avoid; it is hoped that VASI-type units
will be installed without delay at all airports not yet
so equipped. The cost for a twelve-box array is less
than £5,000 ($15,000).

The last SLAET suggestion is of particular interest for it gets to the very heart of the safety problem, as did the personal opinion of R. E. Hardingham, Secretary and Chief Executive Office of Britain's Air Registration Board, who stated: "In my opinion the greatest single contribution to safety is the provision of low speeds for take-off and landing. The demand for high cruising speeds has led to high wing loading and, because speed lowering devices have not kept pace, stalling speeds are much too high." There is no doubt that if current landing speeds were of the order suggested by SLAET, many of the other devices or suggestions put forward would lose their urgency.

It must be emphasized that a low stalling speed, if available, would not always be used. For example, it would be more hazardous to land in gusty conditions at sixty knots than at the 120 knots of current jet airliners. A relatively high landing speed is also safer in high cross winds. However, the great attraction of a really low stalling speed is that it would afford pilots more time, when necessary, to carry out their flight deck duties, to observe and to take corrective action. The ability to loiter at sixty knots after breaking cloud in bad weather also offers increased safety.

Is it practical to even think of stalling speeds around the sixty-knot mark? Boeing said that it was not, adding "and still have an economical aircraft".

The increased speed of the subsonic generations of jet aircraft has been achieved largely by means of wing sweep and an increase in wing loading. Very low stalling speeds of the order mentioned could be obtained by one of, or a combination of, three methods:

by increasing the wing area to reduce wing loading; by the use of blown-flaps, that is, flaps over which a jet of air is directed, or blown, to prevent the airflow from breaking away – such flaps develop greatly increased lift; by making use of powered lift, that is, of lift generated directly by power units installed in the aircraft.

Of these three methods, the easiest is the least practical – that of increasing the wing area. With the bigger wing would come increased drag, which would be particularly unwelcome at take-off, as it would require the installation of extra thrust to maintain the margin needed to ensure an acceptable climb performance after engine failure.

The possibility of developing blown-flaps of the required efficiency is more promising. In 1964 Boeing modified their "Dash-80" 707 prototype to incorporate flaps of this type and succeeded in reducing the stalling speed from about 120 to seventy-eight knots. On the Dash-80, the air blown over the flaps was obtained from the main propulsion engines. However, this method introduces a problem in that high engine power levels are required during landing to provide maximum lift while reduced thrust is required to allow a descending flight path. One answer would be to install separate engines to provide the flap air. These could be of the high thrust-to-weight type developed for vertical lift purposes, and would be duplicated to ensure adequate air for blowing.

A great deal of theoretical work has been done on the practicability of using vertical lift engines to give airliners a short take-off and landing capability, which is a function of the lower stalling speeds resulting from the lift engines. When using engine power to generate lift for low stalling speeds, there comes a point when the wings are contributing so little that it is a relatively short step to true vertical flight with engines providing all the lift.

A major problem of low stalling speeds on vertical flight is that of providing adequate control. If the flying speed falls below a certain figure, aerodynamic forces are no longer sufficient, and reaction controls are required which use the thrust of ejected air to provide the controlling force. Much research would be necessary to develop a system of vertical lift engines and reaction controls to the high standard of reliability necessary on passenger-carrying aircraft. The required reliability could probably only be achieved by duplication or even triplication of components, resulting in increased complexity and cost.

A device now in the research stage which might ultimately provide an economic vertical take-off and landing capability for airliners is a "blown" rigid rotor developed by the National Gas Turbine Establishment, Farnborough. In this rotor the lift is produced by blowing a thin sheath of air around a bluff blade section. The rotor could be applied to conventional high speed jet aircraft, on which it would be stopped and parked in cruising flight. A study of such a rotor fitted to the BAC One-Eleven indicates that it could be installed without increasing the number of engines or the engine power, and that the aircraft would be able to hover with one engine inoperative. The aircraft could carry its full passenger complement over short routes, such as London-to-Paris, landing and taking off vertically with noise levels acceptable in densely populated city areas.

A major consideration regarding improvements in air safety is that any manufacturer or airline initiating a safety feature on its own is invariably at a financial disadvantage compared with competitors. For example, there is no doubt that the greatest contribution to increased safety would be, in the famous phrase of the late C. G. Grey, well-known editor of *The Aeroplane*, "aeroplanes that land slowly and not burn up". Yet, when the British Aircraft Corporation took a step in this direction and reversed the trend of ever higher take-off and approach speeds with the VC-10, the significant reduction of some twenty knots was completely overlooked by vociferous critics who only publicized the fact that the inflight operating costs of the aircraft are higher than its competitors.

Summing up, it seems that there is no one single device or procedure that will provide a dramatic breakthrough in air safety, unless it is the advent of reliable airliners able to take off and land vertically. The improvement required must come from an all-round approach covering everything, from air traffic control to design, from workshop to pilot training. As it is an international problem, results might be achieved by allocating specific lines of investigation and development to individual countries.

Meanwhile, there must be no backsliding, and great efforts must be made to improve crashworthiness and reduce the risk of fire in accidents, so that even if passengers cannot land slowly, at least they do not burn up. Nor must the seriousness of the forthcoming shortage of *experienced* pilots be underestimated, for in many ways safety in the air begins with good pilots.

Statistics are weighted against any reduction in air accidents, so there is no time to lose if we are to have safer flying in the future.

AVIATION IN ITSELF IS NOT INHERENTLY DANGEROUS BUT, TO AN EVEN GREATER EXTENT THAN THE SEA, IT IS TERRIBLY UNFORGIVING OF ANY CARELESSNESS, INCAPACITY OR NEGLECT.

SAFETY IS NO ACCIDENT

Notice displayed in BEA office, London Airport.

Printed in Great Britain by
Cox & Wyman Ltd., London, Reading and Fakenham
Abelard-Schuman Ltd., London, New York and Toronto